CAMBRIDGE LIBRARY COLLECTION

Books of enduring scholarly value

Literary Studies

This series provides a high-quality selection of early printings of literary works, textual editions, anthologies and literary criticism which are of lasting scholarly interest. Ranging from Old English to Shakespeare to early twentieth-century work from around the world, these books offer a valuable resource for scholars in reception history, textual editing, and literary studies.

Personal Aspects of Jane Austen

Early in the twentieth century, public interest in Jane Austen (1775–1817) was considerable. Although the popularity of her work had remained modest in her lifetime, she was sufficiently well known by the centenary of her death to have provoked toxic reviews from Henry James and Mark Twain along with the reserved support of E.M. Forster. Previous biographies had been riddled with inaccuracies: she was called 'narrow', was said to have disliked children and animals, and to have led a quiet, almost monastic life. Many of these mistakes could be traced back to the unashamedly idealised biography written by her nephew, but while contrary accounts emerged later in the form of her letters, the old misapprehensions endured. In this neglected addition to Austen literature, first published in 1920, Mary Augusta Austen-Leigh (1838–1922) corrects many of these errors, advocating a closer critical reading of her great aunt's novels.

Cambridge University Press has long been a pioneer in the reissuing of out-of-print titles from its own backlist, producing digital reprints of books that are still sought after by scholars and students but could not be reprinted economically using traditional technology. The Cambridge Library Collection extends this activity to a wider range of books which are still of importance to researchers and professionals, either for the source material they contain, or as landmarks in the history of their academic discipline.

Drawing from the world-renowned collections in the Cambridge University Library and other partner libraries, and guided by the advice of experts in each subject area, Cambridge University Press is using state-of-the-art scanning machines in its own Printing House to capture the content of each book selected for inclusion. The files are processed to give a consistently clear, crisp image, and the books finished to the high quality standard for which the Press is recognised around the world. The latest print-on-demand technology ensures that the books will remain available indefinitely, and that orders for single or multiple copies can quickly be supplied.

The Cambridge Library Collection brings back to life books of enduring scholarly value (including out-of-copyright works originally issued by other publishers) across a wide range of disciplines in the humanities and social sciences and in science and technology.

Personal Aspects of
Jane Austen

MARY AUGUSTA AUSTEN-LEIGH

CAMBRIDGE
UNIVERSITY PRESS

CAMBRIDGE UNIVERSITY PRESS

Cambridge, New York, Melbourne, Madrid, Cape Town,
Singapore, São Paolo, Delhi, Mexico City

Published in the United States of America by Cambridge University Press, New York

www.cambridge.org
Information on this title: www.cambridge.org/9781108062015

© in this compilation Cambridge University Press 2013

This edition first published 1920
This digitally printed version 2013

ISBN 978-1-108-06201-5 Paperback

PERSONAL ASPECTS OF JANE AUSTEN

Frontispiece]   *[J. Zoffany, R.A., pinxit*

JANE AUSTEN.

PERSONAL ASPECTS

OF

JANE AUSTEN

BY

MARY AUGUSTA AUSTEN-LEIGH

WITH ILLUSTRATIONS

LONDON
JOHN MURRAY, ALBEMARLE STREET
1920

TO ALL
TRUE LOVERS OF
JANE AUSTEN AND HER WORKS
THIS BOOK IS
DEDICATED

CONTENTS

ILLUSTRATIONS

PERSONAL ASPECTS OF JANE AUSTEN

CHAPTER I

INTRODUCTION

JANE AUSTEN was born at Steventon Rectory in Hampshire on Saturday, December 16, 1775, and died in Mrs. David's lodgings, College Street, Winchester, on Friday, July 18, 1817, in her forty-second year.

Little was known by the world in general either of herself or of her surroundings for many years after the latter date. She had named her brother Henry as her literary executor, and in six months' time he published the two novels she had left in manuscript, 'Northanger Abbey' and 'Persuasion' (to which he himself gave these titles), prefixing to the former a short sketch of their author, called a 'Biographical Notice of Jane Austen.'

B

The same 'Notice,' enlarged by a few additional paragraphs, appeared again in 1833, when Mr. R. Bentley, who had acquired the copyright of all her works, brought out a complete edition of the novels, no other edition being published during the first sixty-four years that elapsed after her death. The smallness of the print employed, ill-suited to any but young and strong eyes, may in part account for the slowness with which her fame grew during that period. But though a slow it was a sure growth, and with an increase in the number of her readers came an increased desire to know more details concerning herself.

As curiosity on these points became stronger, while the family remained silent, it was not unnatural that in the absence of definite information certain erroneous ideas should be entertained, and some mistaken statements made respecting herself, her home, and her position and opportunities in life. Reviewers were inclined to assume that her outlook upon the world at large must have been narrow and restricted to a small circle, though chiefly, as it would seem, because they themselves knew little about her beyond the facts that she had been a daughter of the Rector of Steventon, that she had lived in the country, had never mixed in literary circles, and had died almost before reaching middle age. Surprise would sometimes be expressed as to how, under these disadvantageous circumstances, it should have been possible for her to paint the varied pictures of human nature and give the accurate descriptions of contemporary manners with which her books were filled. Again, conjectures were made that these dealt with one class of life only, that of the English gentry, not from choice but from necessity, because she had no knowledge of anything beyond it. It was also reported that ' Jane Austen was not fond of children '—it was left to a modern foreign critic to add that ' She was not fond of animals.'

To some degree, though not entirely, these mistaken ideas were dispelled when, in 1869, the first ' Memoir of Jane Austen ' was published by her nephew, the Rev. J. E. Austen-Leigh. He had been the youngest of the mourners at her funeral fifty years earlier, and many friends, knowing how well fitted he was to write a memoir of his aunt,

had in after years often begged him to undertake this labour of love, which he for long
declined on the score that he had so little to
relate. In saying this he was referring to his
own recollections of the aunt who died when
he himself had hardly reached manhood, and
to the scantiness of the records he possessed
concerning her. At last, however, he con-
sented to make an attempt, and, being much
assisted by the excellent memories of his two
sisters, Mrs. Lefroy and Miss Austen, he found
it possible to complete a 'Memoir of Jane
Austen.' This work must always hold a
unique position as containing the testimony
of those who well knew its subject and of
being absolutely authentic and faithful so far
as the biographer's memory, which was admirable, and those of his sisters could ensure
its perfect accuracy. It could not relate
that which none of them knew, respecting
the details of her earlier life, nor could it
describe many facts given in letters not then
before him, to which later writers have had
access.

The book was rightfully named a 'Memoir,'
as his chief object was to record that which
he himself remembered. Readers would on

their side do well to bear in mind that his recollections ranged only from childhood to very early manhood, and that his Aunt Jane could never have appeared to him as a young person. When, therefore, he speaks of her life as 'domestic' or 'uneventful,' his thoughts were going back only to the quiet years she spent towards its close in her home at Chawton. Of her earlier and gayer experiences, he probably knew nothing, and still less likely was it that, in spite of their strong mutual affection, he should have any knowledge of the intimate and private feelings of an aunt whose years, at the time of her death, numbered more than twice his own.

It is, perhaps, not surprising that contemporary reviewers of the 'Memoir' should, without sufficiently considering these circumstances, have caught up some of his expressions and dwelt upon them, as though they described the whole of her lifetime, and not the latter part only. These writers speak of her life as being 'uniform' and the circle of her experience 'narrow.' They say 'her lifeworld presented a limited experience.' 'It was a simple and uneventful,

monotonous life,' while one critic also gives
it as his opinion that 'the range of her
sympathies was narrow.' 'Miss Austen
lacks the breadth and depth of feeling which
distinguished her great successor, George
Eliot.' Another says, 'a neat, natty, little
artist was Jane Austen,' and yet another,
'When we compare her to George Eliot the
reader will see at once the eminence on
which we place her.'

Such were some of the judgments passed
on Jane Austen half a century ago.

But a considerable amount of additional
information concerning her earlier life and
its surroundings has now been acquired, of
which later biographers were able to avail
themselves. First in order came the 'Letters
of Jane Austen,'[1] published in 1884 by Lord
Brabourne. The existence of these letters
was known to the writer of the 'Memoir,'
but he could not examine them, as their
owner, his cousin, was then too infirm to
undertake the labour of looking through
them and, without having done so, she did
not wish to place them in any other hands.

---

[1] *Letters by Jane Austen*, edited by Lord Brabourne.
(Bentley & Son, 1884.)

They had been written by Jane to Cassandra, and though of high value in supplying a biographer with many facts, are yet a peculiarly restricted selection, which should never be taken as a specimen of her general correspondence, having been spared by Cassandra only in the full belief that they contained nothing sufficiently interesting to induce any future generation to give them to the world. Since the publication of these letters by Lord Brabourne, other letters, written by more distant branches of the Austen family, have been recovered, which bear upon the life at Steventon Rectory in old days, and consequently upon that of Jane herself.

Another book, giving some authentic details of the same, dealing principally with the careers of her sailor brothers,[1] was published in 1916 by a great nephew and niece. All the fresh knowledge thus acquired has been embodied in the latest ' Life of Jane Austen,'[2] which was published in

---

[1] *Jane Austen's Sailor Brothers*, by J. H. Hubback and Edith C. Hubback. (John Lane Co.)

[2] *Life and Letters of Jane Austen*, by W. Austen-Leigh and R. A. Austen-Leigh. (Smith, Elder & Co.)

1913 by a great nephew and a great, great nephew.

So much fresh information having been given to the world respecting Jane Austen's youthful years since the publication of the original ' Memoir,' which dealt almost wholly with her later life, it certainly occasions some surprise to find critics of the present day apparently disregarding these later biographies and reverting to the standpoint of those writers who knew only the earliest. Yet so it is. In a recently published book we again hear of her ' narrow experience,' and are told that she ' lived aside from the world,' also that ' concerning her personal character and private interests we know remarkably little,' and that ' her life provided even less variety of incident than she discovered at Longbourn or Uppercross,' while the same writer states, in spite of all evidence to the contrary, that ' her father was not very much better educated and scarcely more strenuous than his neighbours —nor were there granted to her any of the consolations of culture.'

Since it is still possible for an earnest and acute student of her works to offer, as ascertained facts, views of his own concerning their writer which contain so many misapprehensions, it may be well once more to record a few simple truths about Jane Austen's position in life, her education, and her choice of subjects as an author.

CHAPTER II

POSITION

THAT Jane Austen should take as her field
of work one which, though far from being
narrow, was certainly definite, the life, namely,
of the English gentry, was so natural as
hardly to require either remark or explana-
tion. It was the class to which her ancestors
had for some centuries belonged and with
which she had always associated. The
Austens of Steventon Rectory were descended
from many generations of Kentish Austens
who, arising like other county families from
the powerful clan of Clothiers, known in the
Middle Ages as the 'Gray coats of Kent,'
were, in the sixteenth century, settled as
landowners in two small and picturesque
old manor houses, Grovehurst and Broadford, which still form part of the Austen
property, though the heads of the family
removed long ago to larger habitations and

increased possessions in the parish of Horsmonden, near Sevenoaks, a neighbourhood where the name of Austen has long been known and held in honour. They were a purely English family. No admixture of Scottish, Irish, or foreign blood appears in the pedigree of the Austens of Broadford, which runs back to the close of the sixteenth century.

They were also a race accustomed to prize both religion and education. On the tomb of the wife of the first John Austen, of Broadford (Joan Berry), in Horsmonden Church, dated A.D. 1604, it is recorded that she met her death ' often utteringe these speeches, " Let neither husband nor children nor lands nor goods separate me from my God." ' A hundred years later another Mrs. John Austen existed, whose name (Elizabeth Weller) deserves to be held in perpetual respect and esteem by her descendants. In her portrait, taken when she was a blooming young woman, she appears in brocade and pearls, suitable to the wife of the heir to the estate, and future Lady of the Manor. But the latter position she never held, as her husband died before his father, who, like 'the old Gentleman' in 'Sense and Sensibility,' showed an exclusive care for his eldest grandson and heir, and, soon dying himself, left to his daughter-in-law the task of bringing up on small means her remaining five sons and a daughter. Without repining at her want of fortune, she quickly set to work to give them that which she thought would best supply its absence, namely, learning, and that they might receive a sound classical education, she removed to Sevenoaks, to send them as day-boys to its old Grammar School, and to take some of its masters as lodgers into her own house as an assistance towards defraying the expenses of her large family. She had her reward in living to see her daughter married and all her sons established in different professions. This brave woman was Jane Austen's great grandmother, as her fourth son, William, a surgeon in Tonbridge, became the father of George Austen—he being the first of the race to leave his native county and make a home in Hampshire.[1]

---

[1] Cf. *Chawton Manor and its Owners*, by William Austen-Leigh and Montagu George Knight, Chap. I. (Smith, Elder & Co.)

Steventon Rectory (front).

12]

When he was settled at Steventon, regular communications with the relations he had quitted in Kent were kept up. The Kentish Austens had, naturally, formed many connections by marriage with families in their own county and when Jane, at the age of twelve, had for the first time the delight of going with her parents and her sister into Kent, she would make acquaintance with a number of relations hitherto unknown to her excepting by name—an epoch in life to a girl of that age, gifted with strong family instincts and quick power of observation. It is due to the correspondence maintained between the Hampshire and the Kentish cousins that various facts relating to the period of Jane Austen's girlhood were not long ago discovered by one of the authors of 'Life and Letters.'

None of these early letters were written by Jane herself, but in later life it was her custom to write many to relations at a distance, thus acting up to a remark she once made to a niece, 'I like cousins to be cousins, and interested in one another.'

This hereditary interest was also felt to the full towards the maternal side of the house, where the young George Austens' descent was of an interesting and varied character. Mrs. George Austen had been Cassandra Leigh, one of the Leighs of Addlestrop in Gloucestershire, an elder branch of the Leighs of Stoneleigh in Warwickshire, to which property they succeeded when the junior line died out. All came from the family of Leighs, who were settled at Highleigh in Cheshire from the date of the Norman Conquest. Early in the reign of Henry VIII one of these, Thomas Leigh, came when a lad to seek his fortune in London. In this quest he was highly successful and was knighted by Queen Elizabeth, being Lord Mayor of London in the year of her accession, 1557. As such he had the honour of receiving her and preceding her, carrying the sceptre before her Grace when she first entered the City to take up her residence at the Tower. He also bore a leading part in the ceremonies of her Coronation in the following year. Romantic incidents and stirring events belong to the history of Sir Thomas Leigh's descendants, who must have possessed much determination, strength of character, and keen sense of humour. They were also noted for inflexible loyalty to the

House of Stuart through every change of
fortune that befell its monarchs. When
Charles I was on his march to Nottingham,
there to set up the Royal Standard, he found
on reaching Coventry that the gates of that
city were closed against him by order of the
Mayor. On this he rode off to Stoneleigh
Abbey, where he and his escort were hospitably
received by the reigning Sir Thomas Leigh, a
grandson of the original Sir Thomas. Again,
in 1745 apartments were prepared in the
Abbey which, it was hoped, that Charles
Edward would occupy for at least one night;
but he was not destined to enjoy such comfortable quarters in England, and very fortunate beyond a doubt was it for the Leighs
that he retreated without reaching the mid-
land counties. To Jane Austen, who was,
as will be shown further on, a most worthy
descendant of the 'loyal Leighs,' every story
or relic connected with these historic
memories of the Stuarts must have been
deeply interesting, when she spent some
time at Stoneleigh Abbey in August 1804;
and greatly indeed would her delight have
been increased could she have beheld a
remarkable family treasure which the house

then contained, the very existence of which was at that time unknown, and so remained for another twenty years. It was in 1827 that Sir George Beaumont, well known as a connoisseur in art, when examining a flower-piece in oils at Stoneleigh Abbey, detected what appeared to be a human eye looking at him from amongst the flowers. On further examination it was ascertained that these had been thinly painted over another picture, and when they were removed a fine portrait of Charles I by Vandyke came to light. This method of concealment, adopted no doubt to save the picture from the thrust of some Parliamentary pikestaff, had proved so effectual that not even a tradition of the portrait had survived. It must have lain hidden for nearly two centuries until chance, as in the case of 'The Bride of the Mistletoe Bough,' revealed the long-kept secret, and the fine painting, happier in fortune than the ill-fated bride, emerged again in all its pristine beauty. Stuart monarchs have been accused of ingratitude towards their followers, but here, on the contrary, it is a pleasant, as well as a probable, theory that the portrait was sent to Sir Thomas Leigh in token of the gratitude felt by a King who had been sheltered by him in a time of need.

It was through her Leigh relations that Jane became, while still young, well acquainted with Bath. Cassandra Austen's brother, James Leigh (Perrot), himself a man of good fortune, had married a well-endowed lady, Miss Cholmeley, from Lincolnshire. They possessed a country home in Berkshire, and had also, as a winter residence, a house in Bath, No. 1, Paragon, commanding a lovely and extensive view. There they lived as people of fashion and fortune in the later years of the eighteenth century, and parts of beautiful old costumes worn by them still exist to show how brilliant must have been the scenes then presented by the gay world of Bath. The Leigh Perrots, who were childless, received their Steventon relations as visitors, and the eldest of Cassandra's sons was generally looked upon as his uncle's natural heir.

Through circumstances which befel her next brother, Edward (Knight), Jane had again a fresh and a wide view of English society opened to her observation. Edward had been adopted, while still a young boy,

c

by another childless couple, Mr. and Mrs.
Thomas Knight, who were cousins on the
Austen side of the house, and possessors of
large properties both in Hampshire and in
East Kent. It was in the latter neighbourhood that Edward married and settled, at
first in a home of his own, whence he removed
after Mr. Knight's death to the large house
and beautiful estate of Godmersham Park,
near Canterbury, and in East Kent, Jane, as
a young woman, began to visit her brother
Edward and his family. Visits, like the
journeys that led to them, were in those
days long affairs, and hers must have afforded
ample time as well as opportunity to mix
in the society of that neighbourhood,
where she could observe English county life
from a fresh point of view, and could compare
it with the corresponding class of society
she already knew well in Hampshire around
Steventon. The share taken in the latter
by the George Austens has been thus described
by the author of the original ' Memoir.'
He says : ' Their situation had some peculiar
advantages beyond those of ordinary
rectories. Steventon was a family living.
Mr. Knight, the patron, was also proprietor

of nearly the whole parish.   He never resided
there and, consequently, the rector and his
children came to be regarded in the neighbourhood as a kind of representatives of the
family.   They shared with the principal
tenant the command of an excellent manor
and enjoyed, in this reflected way, some of
the consideration usually awarded to landed
proprietors.   They were not rich, but, aided
by Mr. Austen's powers of teaching, they
had enough to afford a good education to
their sons and daughters, to mix in the best
society in the neighbourhood, and to exercise
a liberal hospitality to their own relations and
friends.   A carriage and pair of horses were
kept. . . . The horses probably, like Mr.
Bennet's, were often employed in farm work.'

From the foregoing account it will be
evident that to place, as has been done by
a recent critic, Jane Austen and Charlotte
Brontë together in one sentence, as both
'living aside from the world,' is entirely
wide of the mark.   Beyond the facts that
their fathers were clergymen and that both
lived in the country, no resemblance whatever can be discovered in their situations,
which were as unlike as were their several

characters. No counterpart to the isolation and sadness of Haworth Rectory could be found in the happy and sociable atmosphere of the Rectory at Steventon. Her nephew, who well knew those of whom he wrote, says in his original ' Memoir ' : ' There can be no doubt that the general colouring of Jane Austen's early life was bright. She lived with indulgent parents in a cheerful home, which afforded an agreeable variety of society.' Jane, like most young girls, thoroughly enjoyed the gaieties of the neighbourhood around her, of which dancing formed a great feature. Her brother Henry says : ' She was fond of dancing and excelled in it.' It may be remembered that nearly all her heroines shared in this taste—even the timid Fanny feeling that a ball ' was indeed delightful.' That Jane Austen was in every way well fitted to write of the lives and feelings of English gentle-people is not to be questioned, nor that this would be a determining factor in directing her imagination towards such a field of work. It is not, however, a proof, as may be shown later, that there was none other at her command had she thought well to choose it.

CHAPTER III

EDUCATION—I

CASSANDRA and Jane Austen, while still children, must have had a larger acquaintance with the world than can usually fall to the lot of such young girls. Space was probably needed within their own home for the reception of George Austen's pupils, and his little daughters, at the ages of nine and six, were sent to be educated elsewhere, not, as we are told, because it was supposed that Jane at six years old required very much education, but because it would have broken her heart to be separated from Cassandra. The sisters, therefore, went together to Oxford, there to be placed under the care of Mrs. Cawley, who was a connection of their mother and the widow of a Principal of Brasenose College ; a lady of whom no record remains beyond the fact that she was a stiff - mannered person. Mrs. Cawley removed after a time to Southampton, and by so doing very nearly put an end to Jane's short existence, for in that town both she and Cassandra fell very ill of what was then called ' putrid fever,' and Jane's life was at one time despaired of. Mrs. Cawley would not at first write word of this illness to Steventon Rectory, but Jane Cooper, the little girls' cousin, who was one of the party, thought it right to do so, an action which was probably instrumental in saving the life of Jane. Mrs. Austen at once set off for Southampton together with her sister, Mrs. Cooper, and they brought with them a remedy, to the use of which Jane's recovery was ascribed. But a heavy price had to be paid for this blessing. Poor Mrs. Cooper took the infection herself and died at Bath, whither she went on quitting Southampton. Such a tragical time must have remained fixed in any child's memory, and in the delirium and distress of Marianne Dashwood, when lying dangerously ill at Cleveland, also of a ' putrid fever,' and also awaiting the arrival of a mother, we probably hear an echo of poor little Jane's delirious entreaties for her own mother, when lying

equally ill in the strange world of Southampton.

The next experience of the sisters was of
a happier nature. They and their cousin,
Jane Cooper, spent two years in the kindly
Abbey School at Reading, with its beautiful
garden and picturesque old buildings. From
all accounts, discipline here was not of a
rigid order, for when their brother and
cousin, Edward Austen and Edward Cooper,
were passing through Reading Cassandra
and the two Janes were allowed to dine with
them at an inn in the town. A charming
fancy drawing of this happy young party
has been made by Miss Ellen Hill.[1] When,
therefore, these early adventures in search
of education came to an end and the sisters
returned to continue their lessons at home,
it must have been with imaginations already
enriched by some acquaintance with the
three old towns of Oxford, Southampton, and
Reading.

At Steventon they would not suffer from
any want of competent teachers. Basingstoke was near enough to furnish whatever

[1] *Jane Austen : her Homes and her Friends,* by
Constance Hill. (J. Lane.)

occasional instructions might be needed from masters, such as Elizabeth Bennet told Lady Catherine could always be had at Longbourn for those who desired them. But the most valuable and solid part of their mental training they must have received in their own home, where they would find excellent opportunities for studying English literature and language under their father, who ceased by degrees to take private pupils into his house, and would, therefore, have sufficient leisure for teaching his own children. The recent critic who spoke of him as being probably 'not very much better educated, and scarcely more strenuous than his neighbours' makes an entire mistake. George Austen had won an open scholarship and fellowship at St. John's College, Oxford, and had been for a time a master at his own former school, Tonbridge, before returning again to reside at St. John's as an Oxford Don. In later life he prepared two of his sons for matriculation at the same College, and one of these has thus written of him, with especial reference to the education he gave to Jane. ' Being not only a profound Scholar, but possessing an exquisite taste in every species of Literature, it is not wonderful

Steventon Rectory (back), 1814.

24]

that his daughter Jane should at a very early age have become sensible of the charms of style and enthusiastic in the cultivation of her own language.' We may, perhaps, allow for a little filial exaggeration here, but we should also remember that it is first-hand evidence, coming from one of George Austen's own pupils. That he would be a kind and welcome instructor is certain from the way in which Jane afterwards recalls his strong affection for his family, his 'indescribable tenderness as a father,' and 'the sweet, benevolent smile which always distinguished him.' To learn of such a teacher must have been a constant pleasure, and she had another assistant at hand in her eldest brother James, himself a classical scholar and a cultivated man, of whom his son, the author of the original 'Memoir,' thus writes: 'He was well read in English literature, had a correct taste, and wrote readily and happily both in prose and verse. He was more than ten years older than Jane and had, I believe, a large share in directing her reading and forming her taste.' He was also a good French scholar, spending some months in France to perfect himself in the language.

Perhaps Jane remembered this brother's assistance when she made Edmund Bertram perform the same kind offices for his little cousin, Fanny Price.

One glimpse of Jane at her lessons has been spared to us by time and may be found in her own handwriting in an old copy of Oliver Goldsmith's 'History of England.' From internal evidence, she must have been reading it for the first time, with an excited interest that would recall Marianne Dashwood's enthusiastic soul rather than Catherine Morland's indifference to history, where she found 'the men all so bad, and hardly any women at all.' Jane's age can only be guessed at, but from the nature of the remarks she inscribes on the margin of this work, twelve or thirteen years seems a probable time of life for her to have then reached. It was the History of the Rebellion that stirred her loyal soul to its depths. At first she contents herself with these short interjections on the behaviour of Cromwell's party—

' Oh! Oh! The Wretches!'

but she grows eloquent when Goldsmith delivers his verdict against the whole family of Stuart, and cries out in answer—

'*A family who were always ill-used, BE-TRAYED OR NEGLECTED, whose virtues are seldom allowed, while their errors are never forgotten.*'

It is perhaps fortunate—in case some destructive critic should arise in the future to declare the improbability of Jane Austen having written any such words—that a postscript has been added to this note by a sympathetic young nephew, into whose possession the book afterwards passed : ' Bravo, Aunt Jane !   Just my opinion of the case.'

At the conclusion of Walpole's speech her remark is slightly ironical—

'*Nobly said !   Spoken like a Tory !*'

And, again, when Goldsmith refers to the King as a Master unworthy of faithful followers, come these words—

'*Unworthy, because he was a Stuart, I suppose—unhappy family !*'

Lord Balmerino's execution in 1745 is thus lamented—

'*Dear Balmerino !   I cannot express what I feel for you !*'

On the subsequent change in the dress of the Highlanders she writes—

'*I do not like this.   Every ancient custom*

ought to be Sacred, unless it is prejudicial to Happiness.'

Next comes a very sapient announcement. Goldsmith having condemned those who were ' Stunning mankind with a cry of Freedom,' Jane thus addresses him—

' *My Dear Mr. G—, I have lived long enough in the world to know that it is always so.'*

Here she was probably thinking of the French Revolution, in which all at Steventon had a special reason for taking very deep interest.

She did not approve of Anne leaving her father's cause to side with her brother-in-law, and, being unwilling to blame any Stuart, finds her own way out of the dilemma—

' *Anne should not have done so, indeed I do not believe she did.'*

In writing of James II's obstinate adherence to his own policy, Goldsmith refers it to this King's conviction that ' nothing could injure schemes calculated to promote the cause of heaven,' on which Jane observes—

' *Since he acted upon such motives he ought not to be blamed.'*

It must be left to those critics who have described Jane Austen's disposition as ' calm',

as ' unemotional,' ' unsentimental,' ' passion-
less,' to reconcile such epithets with these
eager outpourings, which are given here for
the benefit of all who may care to form some
truer conception of the real Jane than the
tame and colourless personality, devoid of
all enthusiasm and ardour, which has at times
been set before the public as hers, though
something better than this might, one would
think, have been divined from the characters
of her favourite heroines, Emma Woodhouse
and Elizabeth Bennet, neither of whom can
well be decried as wanting in high spirit or
liveliness of nature.

Of Jane's accomplishments in music and
drawing we know little more than can be
found in her brother's notice. He says:
' She had not only an excellent taste for
drawing, but in her earlier days evinced
great power of hand in the management of
the pencil. She was a warm and judicious
admirer of landscape, both in nature and
on canvas. At a very early age she was
enamoured of Gilpin on the Picturesque,
and she seldom changed her opinion either
on books or men.' None of her efforts
in drawing have survived, though a few of

Cassandra's slight water-colour portraits still exist, and also some pencil sketches taken by others of the family, showing that a general love of drawing existed amongst them, in which Jane very probably shared. Her delight in beautiful scenery was so great that she thought it must hereafter form one of the joys of heaven. As regards music, her brother says she 'held her own musical attainments extremely cheap.' They were, of course, not remarkable, but she was the most musical of an unmusical family, and a niece, when writing of her, says she had a natural taste for music. A manuscript music book of hers is still preserved at Chawton, containing, in exquisitely fine writing, some of the songs she used to sing.

How large a share Mrs. Austen may have taken in the intellectual part of her daughters' education we do not know, but she may no doubt be credited with the charge of two important departments—writing and needlework. She herself wrote an admirable hand, both powerful and interesting, rivalling, though not much resembling, that of her daughter Jane, the beauty of whose writing many of her readers know. Jane herself

30] FROM THE STEVENTON REGISTER.

1. Written out by Jane Austen and signed by her Father, 1800.
2. Written out and signed by her Father, 1776.

looked upon good handwriting as an art to be carefully cultivated. She alludes to it more than once in her notes to a little niece, Caroline Austen, and of her nephew Edward Austen's writing she says: 'I am quite happy to see how his hand is improving. I am convinced that it will end in a very gentlemanlike hand, much above Par.' Good writing was general in Jane's home, and those who study caligraphy as a key to character might be interested by finding signs of imagination, grace of mind, and other pleasant qualities repeated in the various scripts.

Good needlework was in their time an accomplishment of great importance in every household, and this their mother would certainly teach them, for she was herself a proficient in it even to the close of a very long life, and her daughters were her imitators. The only time Jane ever bestows *serious* praise upon a performance of her own is when she writes word from Rowling, her brother Edward's first home in Kent, that they are 'all very busy making shirts, and I am proud to say that I am the neatest worker of the party.' No one who has seen the specimens of her needlework

which still exist can doubt that the praise
was well deserved. One of these, which
looks as if it were fashioned by fairy fingers,
is a tiny housewife containing needles an
inch in length, made for a friend by Jane
at the age of seventeen. Another, belonging
to later years, is a scarf of Indian muslin,
two and a half yards long, embroidered
throughout in white satin stitch, its delicate
beauty being unmarred by a single fault.[1]
Equally industrious was she in humbler
tasks. Her niece Anna has written of her
aunts as constantly sitting together, making
clothes for the poor, and varying their occupation by here and there teaching a boy or
girl to read, Jane very probably instructing
a god-daughter of her own, whose father was
coachman to her brother James Austen.[2]

Let those who have done the same declare
whether this shows any interest in their
poorer neighbours or not! Yet a foreign

---

[1] The pattern of this scarf has been produced on the
covers of Miss Hill's book, and also been carved on
the oaken margin surrounding the tablet which was
erected through their exertions on the wall of Chawton
Cottage, in 1917, to commemorate the Centenary of
Jane Austen's death.

[2] See Miss Hill's book, Chap. I.

admirer of her works has not hesitated to charge her with indifference to the needs of the poor, with visiting them as seldom as possible, and with never doubting that they had been created in order that they might serve and respect 'their betters,' adding 'Grief and poverty shock her, as offensive to her taste, things which she forgets as quickly as possible,' and 'she always turns away from suffering, sadness, and ugliness.' Of such a character could it ever have been said that 'to know her was to love her?' The only train of thought in this critic's mind appears to be, 'She did not write of the poor, and therefore she did not care for them.' Jane has, however, left an unconscious contradiction of such imputations on the margin of her Goldsmith, who in one place has described the extreme destitution of the poorer classes after the Revolution, in consequence of which a man and his wife committed suicide. On this her comment is ready—

'*How much are the poor to be pitied, and the Rich to be Blamed!*'

The baseless accusation that she always turned away from whatever was sad,

D

unpleasant, or painful, cannot be allowed to pass unnoticed. One simple instance to the contrary (among many) is described in a family letter. During their residence at Chawton Cottage a general outbreak of measles took place among the Frank Austens, who were at the time inhabiting the Great House. As some relief to the overworked nurses at the House, Miss Gibson, a sister of Mrs. Frank Austen, who was one of the party, was invited over to the Cottage to have *her* attack of measles there, and Mrs. Austen, in a letter to her grand-daughter Anna, thus sums up the result : ' She wanted a great deal of good nursing, and a great deal of good nursing she had,' the nurses being Cassandra, Jane, and their friend Martha Lloyd. Anna, when recording this incident merely adds: ' It was their quiet way of doing great kindnesses.' Jane's powers as a nurse were more severely tried some years later when for many weeks she attended on her brother Henry in an illness in London of which he nearly died.

In returning to the question of early education, it must be pointed out that in the acquisition of foreign languages the

daughters of Steventon Rectory were un-
usually fortunate, often having an excellent
teacher of the same resident for long periods
together under its hospitable roof. This
was their own first cousin on the paternal
side, the Comtesse de Feuillide, Elizabeth
Hancock by birth, who in later life became
their sister-in-law. She was greatly attached
to the family at Steventon, especially to
her Uncle George, and she with her mother
spent much time at the Rectory before she
was taken by the latter to finish her education in Paris, where in 1781 she married a
French nobleman, Jean Capotte Comte de
Feuillide. She was a lovely and accomplished young woman, who went out much
into gay and high society both in Paris and
in London. Her husband's estates were
situated in the south of France, and thither
she at one time travelled, making in the
course of the summer an expedition across
the Pyrenees to take part in the gaieties of
the beautiful watering place, Bagnéres de
Bigorre, on their further side. The affectionate and regular correspondence she maintained with her English relations does not
seem to have been diminished by these

foreign experiences, and when political
thunderclouds gathered over France the
Comte dispatched her, with her infant son,
to England, to find a safe refuge in Steventon
Rectory, where she frequently resided in
the dark days that were to follow, both
before and after the unfortunate Comte
perished on the scaffold in February, 1794.

It was probably in part to Elizabeth that
her younger cousins owed their easy
familiarity with the French language, and
also some knowledge of Italian ; as much,
we may suppose, as Anne Elliot owns to in
' Persuasion.' Whatever the amount may
have been, Jane was tolerably certain, like
Anne, to have decried, as far as possible,
her own personal share in it. But when
she describes herself, long afterwards, to
Mr. Clarke, the Regent's Librarian, as one
who ' knows only her mother tongue and
has read little in that,' and as 'the most
unlearned and uninformed female who ever
dared to be an authoress,' she is indulging
in a flight of fancy and self-depreciation
unusual even for her. It may have formed
the foundation for a strange statement made
by a modern critic that 'if she was fond of

reading, she knew nothing about literature. Her letters do not suggest the uneasiness attached to the possession of a soul—as we moderns understand it.' The connection of these sentences is not very easy to follow, as a large number of persons who certainly know nothing of literature still believe themselves to possess 'a soul,' as that word is usually understood. But the 'modern soul' appears to belong to some distinct order of its own, and thankful may we be that Jane Austen did not possess its 'uneasiness,' for had she done so, we could never have possessed works such as those she has left to the world. Once more, respecting her knowledge of literature, neither here, nor on any similar occasion, is she to be taken at her own valuation. Not only was this honestly a low one, but it suited her playful turn of mind to describe her attainments (excepting in needlework) as even lower than she believed them to be. Thus, when assuring Mr. Clarke of her inability to produce a romance on the whole House of Coburg, the spirit of nonsense evidently rose up within her at the idea, making her add that if, on pain of death, she were forbidden to laugh at herself or other people, she would certainly be hung before she had finished the first chapter. Mr. Clarke may or may not have been capable of a smile here—it must remain doubtful—for there have evidently been other persons of a later date quite unable to perceive when the writer is indulging in the welcome luxury of a pleasant little jest against herself. Her brother's account is altogether different. He says: ' Her reading was very extensive in history and belles-lettres, and her memory extremely tenacious. Her favourite moral writers were Johnson in prose, and Cowper in verse. It is difficult to say at what age she was not intimately acquainted with the merits and defects of the best essays and novels in the English language.'

The predominance given to Crabbe amongst Jane Austen's favourite writers by various annotators is rather singular. It has been due to her joke against herself, preserved by family tradition, and mentioned in the original ' Memoir,' that ' she thought she could fancy marrying Mr. Crabbe,' and on the certain knowledge that she enjoyed his works. But this was no exclusive enjoy-

ment, and he has no place among the poets,
passages from whose works appear in connection with her own heroines. Of these
there are a considerable number. Cowper
was read by Marianne Dashwood and Fanny
Price, the former declaring that his ' beautiful lines have frequently driven me almost
mad.' Anne Elliot studied and discussed
Scott and Byron, and in the laughing choice
of passages from the poets supposed to have
assisted in developing Catherine Morland's
mind, Pope, Gray, Thomson, and Shakespeare
have a place. 'Hamlet' was read aloud in
Mrs. Dashwood's drawing-room, and Henry
Crawford assumes that a knowledge of
Shakespeare is instinctively imbibed from
the atmosphere of every educated household.
A fairly wide acquaintance with English
poets is thus incidentally shown by her
writings, but of Crabbe we only hear that
his 'Tales' lay among the books on Fanny
Price's table.

A pleasant picture of the home circle
to which Jane belonged while still a child,
as it appeared to a visitor in the house,
exists in a family manuscript, written by a
Mrs. Thomas Leigh, who speaks of her cousin

Cassandra as being the wife of 'the truly respectable Mr. Austen,' and says: 'With his sons (all promising to make figures in life) Mr. Austen educates a few youths of chosen friends and acquaintances. When among this Liberal Society, the simplicity, hospitality, and taste which commonly prevail in different families among the delightful valleys of Switzerland ever occurs to my memory.' [1]

[1] *An Old Family History*, by the Hon. Agnes Leigh, *National Review*, April, 1907.

CHAPTER IV

EDUCATION—II

THE general love of literature that prevailed in Steventon Rectory is a sufficient security that Jane could not suffer from any intellectual poverty in her home. In the broader aspects of the word ' education,' she was also fortunately placed. The thoughts of her family were bounded by no narrow horizon. They had private as well as public reasons for taking a deep interest in important matters then agitating the nation at large. While Jane was still quite young the elders of the family could not, if they would, have refrained from following with close attention the great political drama being played out at that time in another hemisphere. The then very far off land of India was brought near to them, and they were familiarised with many details of Indian life through the marriage of George Austen's

only surviving sister, Philadelphia, to Saul
Tysoe Hancock. Mr. Hancock had been
a companion and early friend of Warren
Hastings before his own marriage took place
at Calcutta, and after that event he and
Philadelphia lived on terms of close intimacy
with Hastings, who became god-father to
their only child, Elizabeth. His own only
child had been placed with the George
Austens, and to their great grief had died
as a young boy when still under their care.
Intercourse between Steventon and Calcutta
remained, nevertheless, unbroken ; the trial
of Warren Hastings was followed with the
deepest interest at the Rectory, and when
the impeachment of the latter (begun in
1788) was concluded by an acquittal in 1795,
great were the joy and exultation felt by
his friends in Hampshire.

Of the letters that must have passed
on the occasion only one is extant, coming
from the fluent pen of young Henry Austen,
who addresses Hastings with respectful
devotion and celebrates the great event in
many magnificent phrases. Jane, who was
twenty years old in December, 1795, would
have heard much of Warren Hastings all

her life, and cannot have failed to take a
part in the excitement and enthusiasm felt
by the whole family. Neither was India
the only foreign land with which the George
Austens were personally concerned. The
troubles already arising in distracted France
must have claimed an even greater share
of their anxious attention, since they so
closely affected their own nearest relations.
Many must have been the stories, both gay
and grievous, told by the young Comtesse
and her mother on their return to Steventon,
of life in the French capital at that thrilling
crisis, mixed with descriptions of French
château life in the south, and accounts of
the gaieties of the fashionable world of
Paris at the court of Louis XVI. Another
view of foreign society would also reach
the George Austens through their son,
Edward, who, having been when a young
man entirely adopted by the Thomas Knights,
was sent by them, not to a University, but
to make the then fashionable 'Grand Tour
of Europe.' In his case this included a year
spent in Dresden, where he was kindly
received at the Saxon court. Many years
afterwards, when his two eldest sons had

spent some time in that city and had, like their father, received marks of attention from the Royal Family, there was a pleasant exchange of letters and presents between Prince Maximilian of Saxony and 'Edward Knight, *ci-devant* Austen.' The educational tour of the latter was afterwards extended to Rome.[1] Its date was probably 1786–88, and it comprehended a view of that old Europe soon to be changed by the convulsion of wars and revolutions. Edward, on his return home, would have much to relate of deep interest at Godmersham and Steventon ; Jane being at this period twelve or thirteen years old.

Nor should it be forgotten that while every intelligent and patriotic Englishman must have been following the events in the British fleet with unbroken interest, the Steventon party had a double reason for so doing, since two of George Austen's sons were beginning their careers and hazarding their lives in those naval actions upon the success of which the safety of the whole nation depended.

We see, then, that at Steventon Rectory an ample supply of food for the mind, the

[1] Cf. *Chawton Manor and its Owners*, Chap. VII, p. 158.

heart, and the imagination was furnished
both by public events and by private
interests, and some expressions used by
Jane in later years show that the girl of
twelve or thirteen, whose comments on the
course of English history, occurring a century
or more before her own birth, we have been
reading, remained to the end of her life
a firm patriot and a strong believer in the
superiority in the ways and the merits of
her native country over those of other lands.
In a letter written to an old friend a few
months before her death, she says : ' I hope
your letters from abroad are satisfactory.
They would not be satisfactory to *me* I
confess, unless they breathed a strong spirit
of regret for not being in England.' Yet
critics have arisen, ready to accuse her of
possessing only narrow sympathies and little
patriotism, on the sole ground that no discussions on public affairs, or on the war
with France, appear in her private, intimate
correspondence with her sister Cassandra.
Here we have once more the old cry ' She
did not write of them, *therefore* she did not
care for them.' The falseness of such an
argument, when it attacks a belief in the

kindness of Jane Austen's heart has, it is
hoped, been already shown—but the second
charge, if somewhat less offensive, stands
on no securer foundation than the first.
Why *should* she write of public affairs unless
their sailor brothers' personal histories were
at the moment affected by them? Then
indeed her pen is always active; but on
public issues let us judge her by ourselves.
Our war of five years' duration is just over;
how many sisters, when a lapse of two or
three years had familiarised them with the
thought of its existence would have discussed it, in its public bearings, in letters
to each other devoted to home details?
Yet might they not justly resent an imputa-
tion that the absence of such discussions
proved any want of ardent patriotism on
their own parts? But to Jane Austen, war,
far from being a new and unheard of horror,
was an almost normal state of things. *Her*
England had during a large portion of her
short life been constantly at war. The
gravity of the situation could never be forgotten, but the recent excitement of our
own country, fed as it has been by telegrams
and journalists, did not exist a hundred years

earlier, when intelligence of great battles was
often long in reaching England. Such news
might take weeks on its journey, and private
information was still longer on the passage
home. Francis Austen was made a post
captain in consequence of gallantry shewn in
a naval action in the Mediterranean, but he did
not hear of his promotion until six months
after the action had been fought, the necessary
details having taken three months to travel
home to England, while another period of
three months was required to bring news
of such promotion back to himself.

Nor is it accurate to say that Jane makes
no mention of the war to Cassandra ; it is
referred to more than once, even in the few
fragments of her letters that we possess.
One passage may be cited, and also inter-
preted, to exculpate the writer from any apparent want of feeling on account of the words
she employs : ' May 21, 1811. How horrible
to have so many people killed ! And what
a blessing that one cares for none of them ! '
The action here alluded to is no doubt
Albuera—a very bloody battle, and among
the regiments which suffered most was that
of the ' Buffs ' from East Kent. It is prob-

able that this contained some Godmersham friends and that the object of her remark was to express satisfaction that none of them were among the dead.

Considerations such as these may, perhaps, have some weight in causing critics to hesitate before accusing Jane Austen, on negative evidence only, of narrow sympathies, or any other deficiency. There is also a further reflection which might have checked any writer in drawing conclusions from such of her letters as have been published, but it is one from which the bulk of her commentators turn away, being apparently reluctant to accept the plain account given by a member of her own family, to whom all the attendant circumstances of the occurrence he relates were perfectly well known. Once more let a most important fact, already referred to in a previous chapter, be stated ; this being, not merely that the great mass of Jane's letters were destroyed by Cassandra, but that she kept *only* those which she considered so totally devoid of general interest that it was impossible anyone should, at any time, contemplate their publication. These she bequeathed to her niece, Lady

Knatchbull, whose attachment to her Aunt Jane had, she knew, been so intense that letters however trifling would be loved by her even for the sake of the handwriting alone. Not only, therefore, in quantity, but —which is far more important—in quality, these letters are entirely unworthy specimens of her correspondence in general. They are but ' a gleaning of grapes when the vintage is done '—when all that was precious had been safely gathered up, and garnered in Cassandra's faithful memory, and nothing had been left behind excepting that which even she deemed to be altogether negligible. How vain, then, must be any attempt to extract from this unvalued remainder that wine of the spirit with which all the spontaneous and uncensored works of Jane Austen's imaginative soul are richly filled!

The mistake already referred to made by a recent writer, relating rather to her family than herself, must be once more noticed, as it concerns the subject of her education. Being, as it would seem, unaware of the considerable amount of learning possessed by Jane's father, and passed on by him to his children, he pities her for a want

E

of ' culture ' in her own home, together
with the lack of opportunities by which
she might have ' sought for its consolations '
in some larger sphere. He asserts without
hesitation that her life must have been ' in
a measure isolated, from superiority. She
gave more than she received. Nor can we
believe her entirely unconscious of what life
might have yielded her in more equal companionship.' That ' the highest mounted
minds ' are compelled to fulfil their separate
missions in noble solitude, is no doubt true.
Eminent pioneers of abstract intellectual
effort must necessarily be in advance of other
minds—

' Voyaging through strange seas of thought
        Alone for ever.'

So is it also in the world of imagination.
Every possessor of true creative genius,
having received his separate inspiration, must
as an artist dwell alone with his work, in
which no other human being can claim a
share. But this is a totally distinct thing
from the isolation here declared to have been
experienced by Jane Austen in daily life,
because she had an unavoidable sense of

mental superiority to all her companions. Nothing can be more opposed to every family record and all inherited knowledge than such a conjecture as this. Far from deeming herself to be the intellectual superior of those around her, she sincerely believed to the end of her days that her sister was much wiser and better informed than herself. Her brother Henry writes : ' She had an invincible distrust of her own judgment.' ' She shrank from notoriety.' ' No accumulation of fame would have induced her had she lived to affix her name to any productions of her pen.' To imagine Jane Austen appearing as an authoress in any literary circle, in ' search of the consolations of culture ' is indeed a strange idea, as unimaginable to later generations of her family as it would have been to her own. To live quietly at home and remain unknown as a writer of fiction, was her great wish, and the secret was carefully kept by all her relations until it was at length revealed by the irrepressible Henry himself. Her thoughts and words on this occurrence are already recorded, and they are like herself.[1] So also are the

[1] *Life and Letters*, Chap. XVI, p. 281.

only regrets she ever expressed regarding
shortcomings in education to be found in
her home, these being directed entirely
against herself, and not at all against other
people. She ' wished she had written less
and read more before the age of sixteen.'
Her father's library must have contained
books amply sufficient for the purpose, as,
when quitting Steventon, he left five hundred
volumes to be sold, in addition to those he
may have taken away with him. Jane also
had to dispose of her own modest collection
of books, which was sold for eleven pounds.
In respect to her own characteristic self-
criticism, we may remember that book-
learning does not form the whole of education, and that the facility for writing clear
English, which by a constant use of the pen
she acquired very early in life, together with
the formation of a humorous style, were to
prove in her case invaluable attainments.
All the family could write light, amusing
trifles in verse,[1] some of which had considerable merit, and Jane's childish absurdities
with their solemn dedications to one or other
of the party would, no doubt, be well received

[1] Cf. Appendix, ' Charades.'

as the kind of productions naturally to be
expected from a droll and merry little
sister. When the character of her writings
changed with advancing years, and they
became secrets not lightly to be revealed
to critics downstairs, she was equally fortunate in the possession of one favourite
and favoured listener. A genial atmosphere of warm and encouraging sympathy
is much needed to foster the developing
shoots of romantic authorship, and of this
she was secure in the companionship of
Cassandra, who, while able to form and main-
tain opinions of her own, felt the strongest
possible admiration and enthusiasm for her
sister's works. One of their nieces, writing
in 1856, speaks of having met ' a most ardent
and enthusiastic lover of Aunt Jane's novels,'
and adds : ' *Aunt Cassandra herself would be
satisfied at her appreciation of them ;* nothing
ever like them, before or since.' This niece's
brother, the first Lord Brabourne, who was
sixteen when Cassandra Austen died in 1845,
has thus written of her : ' From my recollections of " Great Aunt Cassandra," in her
latter days, she must have been a very
sensible, charming, and agreeable person.'

Had she been less than this she could hardly have filled Jane's sisterly heart with such absolute satisfaction, respect, and admiration as we know to have been the case, and if further testimony to the strength and beauty of Cassandra's character is needed, it may be found in the letters written by Cassandra herself, immediately after Jane's death, to their niece, Fanny Knight.[1]

No sense of isolation or unfulfilled longings can have troubled Jane's soul when she had Cassandra beside her, and another and an older friend for whom she felt intense love and reverence was also constantly at hand. This was Mrs. Lefroy, of Ashe Rectory, always known in Ashe parish, which bordered on that of Steventon and Deane, as ' Madam Lefroy.' The author of the original ' Memoir ' thus describes her: ' She was a remarkable person. Her rare endowments of goodness, talents, graceful person, and engaging manners were sufficient to secure her a prominent place in any society into which she was thrown ; while her enthusiastic eagerness of disposition rendered her especially attractive to a clever and lively girl.' The notice

[1] *Life and Letters*, Chap XXI.

and encouragement which Mrs. Lefroy
bestowed upon Jane from her childhood
shows her to have possessed quick powers
of discernment, and great was Jane's grief
when this beloved friend died suddenly, in
consequence of a fall from her horse, in
1804. With so perfect an example of good
breeding always before her eyes, and living
continually in the midst of a family whose
manners and bearing towards each other
always struck the next generation as particularly pleasant and harmonious, with the
addition moreover of any information the
Comtesse might occasionally impart concerning what Sir William Lucas would have
termed 'the manners of the great,' Jane
could have no difficulty in learning how to
observe and appreciate in the world at large
those various shades of good breeding, or of
its opposite, which appear again and again in
characters scattered throughout her books.
In one of the most sympathetic and correct
of the shorter works dealing with Jane
Austen that have been published in recent
years, the author has inserted all the correspondence that passed between Mrs. Thomas
Knight and young Edward Austen who was

to succeed her late husband at Godmersham Park. A portion of this appears in ' Life and Letters,' Chap. VI, while the whole of it is of so charming a character that every letter would repay perusal.[1]

On these letters Mr. Pollock makes the following remarks : ' Comment has often been made, and most justly made, on the perfect breeding and manners of those people in Miss Austen's novels who are supposed and intended to be well bred. The object in quoting these letters is to show in what a perfect atmosphere of dignity and good feeling Miss Austen passed her life. There is surely something singularly touching in the sincere affection and the delightful courtesy of this correspondence, and it is certainly most characteristic of the race to which Miss Austen belonged.' The writer, as a resident at Chawton, had enjoyed the friendship of the late owner of Chawton House, Montagu George Knight, Squire of Chawton Manor, and no one who was so happy as to know him can ever have doubted that in courtesy, in charm of personality and

---

[1] *Jane Austen : Her Contemporaries and Herself*, by Walter Herries Pollock. (Longmans & Green.)

CHAWTON HOUSE.

manner, combined with an unfailing kindness of heart, he might well have served as
a model for the highest ideals of his great
aunt, Jane Austen.

In returning to the subject of Jane's education, and taking that word in an extended
sense, one characteristic of the family life
around her ought not to be overlooked,
namely, the strong hereditary love of sport
to be found among its members. George
Austen must have received it from his
Kentish ancestors, for he certainly trans-
mitted it to his descendants, even of a third
and fourth generation. All his own boys
hunted at an early age on anything they
could get hold of, and Jane when five or six
must often have gazed with admiring, if
not envious, eyes at her next oldest brother,
Frank, setting off for the hunting field at
the ripe age of seven, on his bright chestnut
pony Squirrel (bought by himself for £1 12s.),
dressed in the suit of scarlet cloth made for
him from a riding habit which had formed
part of his mother's wedding outfit. Such
early remembrances would be of real advantage to a future novelist, and in the cursory
references to sport occurring in her books we

feel that she is perfectly at home in all branches
of the subject, and could readily enter into
the feelings of Sir John Middleton and Charles
Musgrove towards the precious fox or the
pernicious rat. Nor is it impossible that she
was indulging in a secret smile, born of
remembrance, when Mrs. Jennings exclaims,
' 'Tis a sad thing for sportsmen to lose a day's
pleasure, poor souls! I always pity them
when they do—they seem to take it so much
to heart.'

When the foregoing statements as to
Jane Austen's home, education, and intercourse with society are considered, they will,
it is hoped, put an end to any surprise that
she was so well able to paint the lives of
the English gentry, as well as to every surmise
that she took this class for her subject because
she had no knowledge of anything beyond
it. So far as varied reading, first-hand
evidence, and strong personal interest can
teach us, she was probably better acquainted
with other interesting phases of life than
many young English women of the same
period, age, and station. That any surprise
at her choice of this, for her, most natural
field of work should be felt, is itself the

surprising thing. No one wonders that Miss Edgeworth wrote of Ireland, or Sir Walter Scott of Scotland. Jane Austen was intensely English, by birth and by sympathies. England she loved and of England she wrote ; finding her happiness and interest in the lives of those around her. She might, no doubt, have indulged in romantic flights of fancy with India or France for a background, and filled them with fictitious delights such as were to be found in the fairy tales with which she enchanted her little nieces during their happy visits to Chawton Cottage, but this would have been play work—and her books were to be solid pieces of real work, carefully designed and constructed, polished also with the utmost skill and patience before they could reach the high standard of original invention joined to entire accuracy in minute particulars, which she appears always to have set before herself. In no foreign field of work could she have exhibited that intimate acquaintance with every aspect and detail which her own scrupulous judgment demanded. Vagueness of method, or inaccuracy in particulars, her taste would have condemned as destructive of the true object to be aimed at in fiction. Never having left England herself, she never attempts to convey her characters across the sea, and in one of her letters she warns a young niece who was beginning to compose stories against committing this mistake. Her standard as to the right method by which to captivate the reader's attention and transport him to another world, at once imaginary and real, remains firmly fixed, and the manner in which she attained it affords, as has been well said in another connection, 'an instance of that patient elaboration to which the highest effects in art are due.' Such results can only be obtained where a complete knowledge of the actual goes hand-in-hand with a clear vision of the ideal. Nothing less than first-hand, personal knowledge could satisfy the thoroughness of Jane Austen's nature, or enable her to fulfil, to the utmost of her ability, the imperative requirements of her creative art.

Another highly valuable, and only too rare gift, which she possessed must not be left unmentioned, as it was one in which education bore a share, for 'Nature and

Art both joined' to make her a delightful
and accomplished reader aloud. Her brother
Henry writes : ' Her voice was extremely
sweet. She read aloud with very great
taste and effect. Her own works were
probably never heard to so much advantage
as from her own mouth, for she partook
largely in all the best gifts of the comic
muse.' It may be remembered that when
her mother began to read ' Pride and
Prejudice ' aloud on its first arrival from
London, Jane could not repress a secret
regret that she read it too fast, and did not
always make the characters ' speak as they
should do.' But her own aspirations were
high, for as regarded the stage itself she
owns, ' Acting seldom satisfies me. I think I
want something more than can be.'

Her nephew and first biographer often
formed part of the family party to whom
she would read her novels aloud, and as he
also was endowed with a charming voice
and excellent taste, the few survivors among
the many of those who in former years
listened to his reading can still believe that
they have, through him, heard the tones and
the manner in which Jane Austen was

accustomed to make her characters 'speak as they should do.' Nor did she read from her own writings alone. One of her hearers wrote, as an old man in 1870 : ' She was a very sweet reader. I last heard her when she was on a visit to Steventon. She had finished the first canto of 'Marmion' and had begun the second, when a visitor was announced. It was like the interruption of some pleasing dream, the illusions of which suddenly vanished.'

Nothing has hitherto been said concerning the most important part of the education Jane Austen received in her home—her moral and religious training. It will be found that this is dealt with in the course of the following chapter.

CHAPTER V [1]

MORALITY

Was Jane Austen a Moralist? 'No! many of her fervent admirers will exclaim— 'Thank Heaven—that she was *not!*' Her mission was to amuse, to delight, to refresh us—but neither to reprove nor to condemn us! Those who want 'Moral Tales' must seek them elsewhere; they are not to be found among Jane Austen's writings! They are not, indeed, if to be moral is to be dull, and if no one can instruct without growing tedious. Far, far away from such odious reproaches must those pages for ever shine to which we turn again and again, as beguilers of trouble and companions in mirth, equally welcome in society or solitude, in sickness or health, in early life or in advancing years. They even seem to grow with our growth and strengthen with our strength, for old though

[1] Reprinted by permission from the *Quarterly Review* for October, 1919.

we may be, and wise as we may think ourselves, we never outgrow their freshness or their wisdom. Such is the creed of Jane Austen's earnest adherents. Nor is this all. In addition to the unflagging interest taken in her books by successive generations of readers, a separate interest has grown up in the hearts of many. For them to know her books—in some cases almost by heart—is much, but it is not enough. They desire to know herself also, they seek after a more intimate acquaintance with their unseen lifelong friend, Jane Austen, who, more than one hundred years ago, was laid to rest, early on a summer morning, within the walls of Winchester Cathedral.

The existence of such a feeling came to light as soon as the original ' Memoir of Jane Austen,' already mentioned, was published in 1869 by her nephew, the Rev. J. E. Austen-Leigh.[1] When this book appeared, a singular change took place. It not only brought into being a large number of articles, notices, and reviews concerning its subject and her works, but it also brought to himself a variety of interesting letters from unknown corre-

[1] See Chapter I, p. 3.

spondents, both English and American, describing the effect that its perusal had produced upon the writers' minds. These letters afforded him much pleasure and not a little surprise. Until that period he had not realised to how large a number of readers, and in what a high degree, the Aunt to whom he as a boy and young man had been so warmly attached, had also become a living, though an unseen, friend.

An extract from one of the letters may be given to serve as a specimen of many others : ' Your Memoir has but one drawback—it leaves us with a sad craving for more . . . much as we loved and honoured her before, we love and honour her the more for what you have told us of her, and in the name of my Grandfather, Father, Uncles and Aunts, Cousins and Children, I thank you for your book.'

Words such as these showed that it was not only as an author but as a woman that Jane Austen had made her way into the affections of many readers. Entreaties also arrived that any stories, or fragments of stories, left by her in manuscript might be published, one correspondent urging that

F

'Every line from the pen of Jane Austen is precious.' In response to these warmhearted applications, the writer of the 'Memoir' could do little beyond attending to the last-mentioned request. Having obtained the necessary permission from those members of his family to whom the original manuscripts had been bequeathed by Jane's sister, Cassandra, he included in the second edition of his 'Memoir' 'Lady Susan,' 'The Watsons,' the alternative ending of 'Persuasion,' and some of her childish writings. The reasons why it was impossible for him at the time to do more than this have been already stated—and mention has been made of books subsequently put forth by other members of Jane Austen's family, containing fresh information regarding the external aspects of her history which may in some degree have fulfilled the wishes of the eagerly enquiring readers of the original 'Memoir.'

But though gratified, they may not be wholly satisfied. They may still desire a more intimate acquaintance with her inner self, with those hidden recesses of feeling concerning which a delicate reserve impelled her to keep a very sacred silence. They may long for a sight of the vanished letters, not from idle curiosity, but that, in the words already recorded, ' Much as they loved and honoured her before, they might learn to love and honour her still more.' A natural but a vain wish! The letters perished long ago—sacrificed by Cassandra as an offering of love and reverence to the memory of a sister unspeakably dear to herself.

Yet though in this way we can learn nothing, there is another path, hitherto, we believe, untrodden, by the help of which we may attain a point of view affording us some fresh knowledge respecting those inner convictions Jane Austen was always slow in revealing to the public gaze, and which will at the same time offer a reason for the question at the beginning of this chapter. To accomplish such an object we must turn to her books and reverse our usual attitude of mind towards them by considering each story, not as a separate creation, but as part of a general whole. From an artistic standpoint there is nothing that can tempt us to act in this manner. Every novel is complete in itself, possessing its own plot, characters, and distinctive atmosphere in a remarkable degree. We find scarcely any repetition of ideas among the six, and this may induce the belief that while comparison is easy, combination is impossible, as they possess no similarity among themselves apart from the creative, dramatic, humorous qualities common to all. This is our first, and not unnatural, conclusion. Nevertheless it will be seen on reflection that there is one feature which declares their family likeness. There is one line of thought, one grace, or quality, or necessity, whichever title we like to know it by, apparent in all her works. Its name is—Repentance.

It will be found on examination that this incident recurs in all her novels, neither being dragged in as a moral nor dwelt upon as a duty, but quietly taking its place as a natural and indispensable part of the plot— as an inevitable incident in the formation and development of each successive child of her imagination. Every one, gayer or graver as the case may be, has its own testimony to give on this question, while all display the skill with which the author knew how to handle the subject according to the varying needs of place, character, and surroundings. We shall find that it could not be dispensed with, even in her very early and most lighthearted story, ' Northanger Abbey.' Here the young heroine, under the excitement of wild and captivating romances, allows herself to believe that the man in whose house she is a guest had, not long before, desired, perhaps connived at, the death of his own excellent and charming wife, or, at the very least, is keeping her immured in some dungeon on the premises. Such delusions could not be suffered to go unpunished. Nor were they, but having arisen from nothing worse than wonderful folly, the penalty inflicted is mercifully abridged. Still, the offender has to undergo a period of sharp anguish, brought upon her by a not unreasonable remonstrance on the part of the hero, a son of the supposed villain. Its effect was immediate. ' Catherine,' we read, ' was completely awakened. Most grievously was she humbled. Most bitterly did she cry. She hated herself more than she could express.' But Jane Austen, we are very sure, would never break a butterfly upon the wheel, conse-

quently we learn with no surprise that, after
forming a resolution of 'always judging
and acting in the future with the greatest
good sense,' and being assisted by Henry
Tilney's 'astonishing generosity and noble-
ness of character in never alluding to what
had passed,' Catherine is ready to be con-
soled by 'the lenient hand of time,' which
'did much for her by insensible gradations
in the course of another day,' and that she
has nothing to do but to 'forgive herself and
be happier than ever.' Nevertheless, so
effectually has the work of penitence been
performed that when General Tilney, not
long afterwards, turns her out of his house
at a few hours' notice, she magnanimously
abstains from reverting to her previous sus-
picions that he has at an earlier period either
poisoned or shut up his wife.

Passing from these playful pages to those
of her latest and most pathetic work,
'Persuasion,' we find the same chord struck,
but in a minor key and with a softer tone.
Nothing glaringly wrong could become a
character of whom her own creator wrote
beforehand to a niece 'You may perhaps
like the heroine, as she is almost too good

for me.' Anne Elliot's error was want of
judgment, of too meek a submission to the
direction of an older friend, an error that
'leaned to virtue's side,' and which was
embraced by her unselfish spirit the more
readily because, though destructive of her
own happiness, she was persuaded to believe
that it would promote the future good of a
man whom she devotedly loved. Want of
mental balance and some youthful weakness of character are the worst charges
that can be brought against this almost
perfect being, yet for these she has to suffer
long and to learn, through suffering, the
nature of the mistake she had made.
Repentance, in the form of deep regret,
overtook her as years passed on. 'She
felt,' we are told, 'that were any young
person in similar circumstances to apply to
her for counsel they would never receive
any of such certain immediate wretchedness
—such uncertain future good.' Captain
Wentworth had on his side a worse fault
to repent of. 'I was proud,' he cried, 'too
proud to understand or to do you justice
—too proud to ask you again. This is a
recollection which ought to make me forgive

everyone sooner than myself.' Readers can
only agree with both speakers and rejoice
in the sequel that closes these confessions.

Much graver instances of misconduct and
its subsequent results will be found in the
four remaining novels. Even in the story
written when Jane Austen was quite a
young girl, called first ' Elinor and Marianne,'
and afterwards 'Sense and Sensibility,' the
plot is made to hinge upon the evils inflicted
by the heroine upon herself and her family
through too violent indulgence in a romantic
passion. This renders her indifferent to the
needs and the claims of other people, and
blind to the sorrow of her sister, who is also
suffering in silence from an unfortunate
attachment. It is not until Marianne is
herself in the depths of disappointed affection
that her eyes are opened to the truths around
her. Then—' Oh! Elinor,' she cries, ' you
have made me hate myself for ever. How
barbarous have I been to you!—you, who
have been my only comfort, who have borne
with me in all my misery, who have seemed
to be only suffering for me!' Such is her
first burst of penitence, to be strengthened
by time and a severe illness, after which

she speaks once more: ' I considered the past. . . . I saw in my own behaviour nothing but a series of imprudence towards myself and want of kindness to others. I saw that my own feelings had prepared my sufferings, and that my want of fortitude under them had almost led me to the grave. . . . Had I died, it would have been self-destruction.' The enthusiasm of her self-reproving spirit flows on—to be checked only by resolutions of future amendment, for though as yet unable to believe that her remembrance of Willoughby will ever be weakened by time, she can still add, ' But it shall be regulated, it shall be checked by religion, by reason, by constant employment ' —a resolution sincerely made and faithfully kept.

Repentance in a double form comes before us in the next novel. Nowhere in any of her other writings does it play so conspicuous a part as in ' Pride and Prejudice.' The whole scheme of the book depends upon its being felt, in a very high degree, by the two principal characters, upon its influencing their actions during the last half of the book and leading steadily up to its closing scenes. The late Professor W. Courthope has left a striking analysis of the manner in which this feeling affected the hero of the book and the consequent changes it wrought within him.[1] For this, as for the whole work, he expresses the warmest possible admiration, comparing it, on account of the manner in which ' under a commonplace surface a great artist has revealed a most dramatic conflict of universal human emotions,' to the structure of some grand Greek play. By no other writer can Jane Austen's genius have been dwelt upon with more eloquence or more sympathetic recognition ; but even this appreciation is incomplete, for it contains no reference to the corresponding work of repentance effected in the heroine by the words and actions of the hero. Yet had this been lacking, the perfectly proportioned plot, to which he accords unqualified praise, could never have been constructed and developed. Elizabeth's self-reproach, so soon as she recognises the truth, is not less severe than Darcy's. ' She grew absolutely ashamed of herself . . .

[1] ' Life in Poetry, Law in Taste.' Lectures delivered in Oxford by Professor W. J. Courthope, 1895–1900. Vol. V.

of neither Darcy nor Wickham could she think without feeling that she had been blind, partial, prejudiced, absurd.' ' How despicably have I acted,' she cried, ' I who have valued myself on my abilities . . . how humiliating is this discovery ! . . . Yet how just a humiliation ! I have courted prepossession and ignorance and have driven reason away, where either were concerned. Till this moment I never knew myself.' Again, in a confession to her sister she admits ' I was very uncomfortable, I may say, unhappy, and with no one to speak to of what I felt, no Jane to comfort me and say I had not been so very weak and vain and nonsensical as I knew I had ! Oh ! how I wanted you ! ' Time, by disclosing more of Darcy's real character, could only deepen such regrets and make her grieve over ' every ungracious sensation she had ever encouraged, every saucy speech she had ever directed towards him. For herself she was humbled, but she was proud of him. Proud that in a cause of compassion and honour he had been able to get the better of himself. Darcy's self-condemnation was equally strong. ' My behaviour towards you,' he assures her, 'merited the severest reproof. It was unpardonable. I cannot think of it without abhorrence. . . . The recollection of what I said, of my conduct, my manners, my expressions, is now, and has been for many months, inexpressibly painful to me. . . . I have been a selfish being all my life . . . what do I not owe you! You taught me a lesson hard indeed at first, but most advantageous. By you I was properly humbled.' Such reciprocal repentance and confession could not fail to bring reciprocal forgiveness, and the title of the book ceases to be appropriate before the last page is turned.

Reciprocity in error and penitence were not destined to console the remaining heroine, who falls, entirely through her own fault, into deep distress. Emma Woodhouse, having erred alone, has to endure her burden of remorse in solitude. Every reader will admit that Emma went through vanity further astray than Elizabeth Bennet through prejudice, a verdict foreseen by the author, who, while declaring that how she would be able to 'tolerate those who do not like Elizabeth she does not know,' frankly admits that in Emma she is going to take a heroine

'whom no one will like but herself.' She
did take her, however, to endow her with
that 'nature and spirit' which were dear
to her own heart, and drawing a being, full
of faults, and yet, as Emma's lover believes
at the end, 'faultless in spite of them.'
But justice could not allow this conclusion
to be reached until great vicissitudes of
feeling had been endured. Emma's faults
had inflicted much pain and distress upon
other persons, consequently, at the proper
moment, they had to bring corresponding
wretchedness upon herself. 'Her feelings,'
we are told, after Mr. Knightley's expostula-
tion on Box Hill, 'were combined of anger
against herself, mortification, and deep concern. . . . The truth of his representation
there was no denying. She felt it at her
heart. How could she have been so brutal,
so cruel to Miss Bates!' Far heavier retribu-
tion, however, is still awaiting her when she,
with horror, finds herself obliged to listen to
Harriet Smith's outpourings of hopes and
expectations respecting Mr. Knightley. Then
she saw her own conduct with a clearness
which had never blessed her before. . . .
'What blindness, what madness, had led her

on ! It struck her with dreadful force, and she was ready to give it every bad name in the world. . . . With insufferable vanity had she believed herself to be in the secret of everybody's feelings ; with unpardonable arrogance proposed to arrange everybody's destiny. She was proved to have been universally mistaken ; and she had not quite done nothing—for she had done mischief.' ' What,' in conclusion, ' could be increasing Emma's wretchedness but the reflection, never far distant from her mind, that it had been all her own work ? The only source whence anything like consolation or composure could be drawn was in the resolution of her own better conduct and in the hope that every future winter of her life would find her more rational, more acquainted with herself, and leave her less to regret when it were gone.' Satisfied with such genuine repentance, the author can now permit herself to make this favourite heroine once more happy.

Can we avoid perceiving that these five pictures of life resemble each other in so far that every one of them gives a description, closely interwoven with the structure of

the story and concerned with its principal
characters, of error committed, conviction
following, and improvement effected, all of
which may be summed up in the word ' Repentance ' ?   If so, do we not also through
this perception gain more knowledge as
to the habitual bent of that mind in which
these successive creations arose ? Does not
Jane Austen's outlook upon life grow clearer
to us when we learn that it was not merely
by the ' follies and nonsense, whims and
inconsistencies ' (as she makes Elizabeth
Bennet call them) ever visible on the surface
of society, that her quick eyes were caught,
but that her penetrating gaze went down to
the hidden springs of action, prompting her
to reflect upon the race that all human
beings have to run in this world, upon the
various courses they pursue, and upon the
necessity of powerful influences being
exercised over them, in order to bring about
that improvement of character which is
the final purpose of it all ? Can we fail to
see how, in dealing with these heroines, she
desired to leave them, not only happier, but
better, than she found them ; wiser, stronger,
humbler, and more charitable, richer in

self-control, and in that self-knowledge on which she always places a high value? If we have seen all this, we have seen also something of her hidden self.

There is still another book, standing in some respects apart from the rest, through which we acquire even more information on this subject. 'Mansfield Park' is the gravest novel Jane Austen ever wrote. It was composed after a long interval of silence, and may be called a 'Second First.' It was the result of a wider experience of mankind, together with that of various personal trials which she had to undergo during eight years passed in large towns after quitting Steventon in 1801. She herself when writing this book declared 'it was not half so entertaining as "Pride and Prejudice,"' an opinion with which her readers may or may not agree. In its pages humour, insight into character, creative genius, and power of description shine as brightly as ever, but in addition to these we are aware of a deeper seriousness and a more searching enquiry into the ultimate issues of conduct than had as yet appeared in her works. The author of the original

'Memoir' was informed that a number of well-known literary men who happened to meet at a country house agreed to write down the title of their favourite novel. The only name which appeared more than once was 'Mansfield Park,' and this had been chosen by three or four of the company, while all united in admiring the book. Such a power of attracting powerful minds may be due to the union of brilliant writing with serious reflection which its pages contain, and it is interesting to recall the circumstances under which this novel, the first important original work taken in hand by her for ten years, was written.

The lapse of ten years, beginning in early womanhood, can hardly pass over any head without producing sensible differences. To Jane Austen they had brought many changes, as enumerated in 'Life and Letters.' [1] Sorrow had touched her closely. She had lost through sudden death, and almost simultaneously, her father and her much-loved friend, Mrs. Lefroy of Ashe. The same cause had brought to an end her own personal romance, inflicting a wound which was, as

[1] *Life and Letters,* Chap. **XIV.**

G

we know, not the less but the more likely
to have been deeply felt, on account of the
silence preserved by Cassandra on this subject
for many years after her sister's death, and
the guarded manner in which she at length
alluded to it. Other trials and troubles
had come upon the Austen family in recent
years, one being of a most unusual nature,
threatening to overwhelm some of them in
irretrievable disaster, and to bring lasting
distress upon their whole circle.[1] That such
practical acquaintance with some of life's
heaviest afflictions should for a time stop
all flow of fancy on Jane Austen's part is
not surprising, nor that the only new work
she began during this period should have
been broken off at the end of the twelfth
chapter, apparently because the author
ceased to feel any interest in its contents.
One more loss—this time neither sudden nor
unusual—must be added to those already
mentioned. She had lost her youth. At
the age of twenty-five, while still a young
woman, she had left her native place, her
earliest friends, and every well-loved scene
associated with the first overflowings of her

---

[1] *Life and Letters*, Chap. IX.

happy girlish fancies. It was the birthplace,
not of herself alone, but of many creations,
born to a far longer existence than hers
was destined to be upon earth—all those
characters that live and move for us throughout the pages of her first three novels. Eight
years were to pass before a return to Hampshire would take place, and her own words
have described how much such a period can
include. ' Eight years . . . what might not
eight years do ? Events of every description,
changes, alienations, removals, all, all must
be comprised in it.'¹ The varied events
which this passage of time had held for
herself can hardly have been absent from
her thoughts when she placed such a reflection
in the mind of Anne Elliot, rejoicing no doubt
that it was in her power to restore to that
heroine a happiness which her own heart
might never now know. It is certain that
on beginning a country life at Chawton she
and Cassandra were satisfied to assume to
themselves, too readily as some of their
relations considered, the position of middle-
aged women. It is impossible, however, not
to rejoice at any decision that ensured to

¹ *Persuasion*, Chap. VII.

her a larger amount of quiet leisure for composition, and now it was, after the revision of two earlier works had renewed the habit of writing, that ' Mansfield Park ' was begun in February, 1811, to be finished in June, 1813.

Here we find the theme, never absent from her works, displayed again, and in an acuter form, for in this book we meet with the chief and saddest example of repentance that her pen ever drew—the saddest because, in a sense, the most unavailing. There can be no comparison between any of the cases already mentioned and that of an unhappy father whose ' anguish arising from the conviction of his own errors in the education of his daughters was never to be entirely done away.' Such are Sir Thomas Bertram's feelings as he contemplates a domestic tragedy for which he believes these errors to have been the primary cause. It is not with folly and thoughtlessness that ' Mansfield Park ' deals, but with vice and sin, with misery and degradation ; subjects the writer herself describes as ' odious,' which she touches as distantly and dismisses as rapidly as possible. That she forced herself to write of them at all tends to show that some of the phases of the fashionable life she had been observing around her had impressed themselves so deeply on her soul that her spirit could not rest until she had entered a protest, through the medium of her own dramatic art, against these forms of evil. A record remains which shows that in her opinion this was the only proper method for a writer of fiction to employ. Soon after the publication of the original 'Memoir' its writer received a letter from a well-known clergyman, who stated that he had been intimately acquainted with a lady who had known Jane Austen well, and from whom he had heard much about her. He spoke of ' the tribute of my old friend to the real and true spring of a religion which was always present though never obtruded.' ' Miss Austen,' she used to say, ' had on all the subjects of enduring religious feeling the deepest and strongest convictions, but a contact with loud and noisy exponents of the then popular religious phase made her reticent almost to a fault.' She had something to suffer in the way of reproach from those who believed she might have used her genius to greater effect, ' but ' (her old friend used to say) ' I think I see her now, defending what she thought was the real province of a delineator of life and manners and declaring her belief that example, and not " direct preaching," was all that a novelist could afford properly to exhibit.'[1]

Means such as these when employed by herself are so powerful and speak so plainly that it is difficult to see how to any author the title of ' Moralist ' can be more justly given. Those who object to it in her case, as necessarily implying a double point of view in a writer's mind, destructive of that simplicity of aim which ought to be the inspiring motive of any true work of art, should consider whether there is in ' Mansfield Park ' any evidence that the design of the artist has been cramped by the mind of the moralist. There are, again, others who would disapprove of the terms ' Morality,' ' Moral Precepts,' as falling short of the highest ideals, and implying something that may be only cold and formal, based upon a theory that correct conduct should be maintained because

[1] This lady used to add, ' Anne Elliot was herself, her enthusiasm for the Navy and her perfect unselfishness reflect her completely.

it is in the long run the most likely method of
obtaining success and comfort in this world.
If so, then 'Mansfield Park' may again be
quoted to refute, in its author's opinion,
any such theory, for it contains a strong
protest against worldliness and the ideals
that worldliness upholds, whether in education, marriage, or general society. In this
book she plainly declares her belief that
moral conduct must spring from a deeper
source and cherish a higher aim than this.
She had seen, and would describe, how
little dependence can be placed upon well-
bred decorum and outward propriety unless
they are inspired by religious principles.
The veil of habitual reticence employed by
her on these subjects is here drawn further
back, and the language used is more explicit
than in any of her other books. Sir Thomas
Bertram's self-reproach is addressed to this
very point. He came to feel, we are told,
that 'Something must have been wanting
within.' He feared that principle, active principle had been wanting ; that his daughters
had never been taught to govern their in-
clinations and tempers properly by that
sense of duty which alone can suffice. They

had been instructed theoretically in their religion, but never required to bring it into daily practice. To be distinguished for elegance and accomplishments, the authorised object of their youth, could have had no useful influence that way, no moral effect on ' the mind . . . of the necessity of self-denial and humility he feared they had never heard from any lips that could profit them.'   Again, the term ' Sin ' is given to express flagrant evil. Edmund employs it in his last interview with Mary Crawford, and of her brother we are told that ' though too little accustomed to serious reflection to know good principles by their proper name, yet in his highest praises of Fanny he expressed what was inspired by the knowledge of her being well principled and religious.'

We learn here more of Jane Austen's deep feelings on moral questions than she has expressed elsewhere, but every allusion to them in her other works is in complete harmony with the teachings set forth in the latter chapters of ' Mansfield Park.' When, therefore, we find in the sister volumes the not infrequent words ' principles ' and ' duty ' we should remember how much they imply, and that we have, as already stated, evidence proving her general reticence on these important points to be intentional and not accidental. ' Still waters run deep,' and the uniform though restrained teaching in these books assures us of the steadfastness of conviction respecting the highest subjects on the part of her to whom we owe their existence. The virtues she loves to cultivate in her characters she would certainly seek after for herself ; the ' self-knowledge ' she prizes so highly as a means of improvement she would personally desire for the same reason, nor was there in her that want of humility which prevents some souls from ever acquiring it. All her life she looked up to Cassandra as her superior in wisdom and goodness, and to its very close she esteemed others as better than herself, for on her deathbed she wrote to a nephew, ' God bless you, my dear Edward. If ever you are ill, may you be as tenderly nursed as I have been.   May the same blessed alleviations of anxious sympathising friends be yours ; and may you possess, as I daresay you will, the greatest blessing of all in the consciousness of not being unworthy of their love. *I* could not feel this.'

That she had reflected silently on solemn
questions some expressions in her letters
show us, and one of her elder nieces has
written: ' When Aunt Jane was grave she was
very grave, graver I think even than Aunt
Cassandra.' Such thoughts on her part, and
such an attitude of mind will not appear
improbable when we recall her ancestry
and education. Her father on one side,
her grandfather on the other, had been
excellent and active parish priests. By
precept and by example she had received
both from her stricter mother and her gentler
father the firm religious principles which
governed her throughout life. Mrs. George
Austen writes, on returning from a visit to
London, that in it ' everyone seems in a
hurry,' adding ' 'Tis a sad place, I would
not live in it on any account, one has not
time to do one's duty either to God or Man '
—a verdict that may provoke a smile, but
which serves to show the speaker's conviction
as regards the great object of human life.
George Austen's instructions to his sons
express, as might be expected, the same
belief. In a long letter of advice, written
to the elder of his two sailor sons, Francis,

when the latter first went to sea, ' attention to religious duties ' is given the primary place, and never were they forgotten by him or by his brothers to the close of their long and honourable careers. Round these twin poles, therefore, ' Duty to God and duty to Man,' had Jane Austen been taught that life should revolve, and this it is that she always presupposes would be accepted in a like manner by the heroes and heroines in all her books. Not that she considers them to be ' already perfect.' ' Pictures of perfection,' she owns, ' make me sick and wicked.' No wonder ! She knew human nature too well for it to be possible that she should accept them as faithful portraits, but this is what she wishes to make her own favourite creations aspire towards throughout the course of their several histories.

To some, perhaps to many, it may appear hardly necessary to insist upon all this. ' We have long known,' they would say, ' the moral tendency of her books, and have believed in the firmly religious convictions of the mind that produced them. Why, then, spend so much time on gilding gold or painting the lily white ? ' Two reasons may

be given in answer to this question, the first
and obvious one being that what is evident
to certain minds is not therefore so to all,
and that among the latter class there may be
those who sincerely desire a closer intimacy
with Jane Austen's inner self, and who may,
by taking the novels as a whole, find that
they can come nearer to comprehending
something fresh and fundamental respecting the nature and soul of their author.
But there is a second reason, and not a slight
one. Jane Austen has now more than one
public. Her, novels are read, appreciated,
and reviewed in other countries besides
our own. In France they have recently
been again brought forward in a work of
great ability, by a writer who describes
her as ' une romancière que l'Angleterre
compte parmi ses plus parfaits artistes de
lettres et que l'originalité aussi bien que
le mérite de son œuvre font qualifier d'incom-
parable.' [1] Mlle. Villard gave further proof
of her admiration for Jane Austen's novels
by choosing them as the subject of her

[1] *Jane Austen : sa vie et son œuvre*, par Leonie
Villard, Agrégée de l'Université, Docteur ès lettres (1915),
preface.

thesis when standing for the Doctorial degree
lately bestowed upon her by the Sorbonne.
Her knowledge and enthusiasm could hardly
be surpassed, while the insight and talent
with which her long and important book is
filled can scarcely be overpraised. But
though the merit of the book is great, this
makes it only the more regrettable that the
view taken by its writer of Jane Austen's
character is so mistaken as to be in some
respects exactly the reverse of the truth.
This is especially the case when dealing
with its religious aspect. Mlle. Villard first
asserts that the Church of England was in
the eighteenth century destitute of all religious
fervour, which, in her own words, ' a disparu
pour faire place à l'indifférence,'[1] and then
passes from the general to the particular
by assuming that the same must therefore
be true of Jane Austen's writings, and that,
for the characters she depicts, religion is
merely ' une fait de même ordre que celui
d'observer les règles de la bienséance mon-
daine.' In proof of this statement a remark
of Archbishop Secker, divorced from its
context, is given, no reference being made

[1] Page 235.

to any evidence leaning the other way furnished by English divines, or, above all, by those who employed the natural voice of strong emotion, poetry—though of these there were a considerable number, including such as belonged to the school of religious mystics. Of one of these latter—Norris— Sir F. Palgrave writes that in 1730 his poems had passed through ten editions, ' one proof out of many,' he adds, ' how exaggerated is that criticism which describes that period as devoid of inner life and spiritual aspiration.' [1] It is thus spoken of in ' La Vie,' where it is called cold, formal, concerned with externals only, and destitute of any ' élan vers un au-delà.' Having passed this judgment upon the Church to which Jane Austen belonged, similar conclusions are come to regarding herself. Sermons, it is said, were wearisome to her ; but a love of sermons, as St. Louis told our Henry III. long ago, is not an indispensable element in the religious life. Moreover, Jane Austen herself says : ' I am very fond of Sherlock's Sermons, and prefer them to almost any.' It is also asserted that she took no interest in anything outside

[1] *The Treasury of Sacred Song*, Note CXLIX.

'a series of traditional rites,' as the services of her Church are called, and that she as a writer 'éloigne de son observation la souffrance, la tristesse et la laideur,' proving that, as a woman, she cared nothing for the sorrows and wants of the poor. Other entire misapprehensions of her nature are also evident, but being concerned with points of comparatively minor importance these need not be entered upon here. The sum total, however, represents a narrow nature, with a heart cold towards God and unsympathetic towards man, somewhat contemptuous of the needy and ignorant and caring little for any fellow creatures beyond those of her immediate family circle. Easy indeed is it to prove the contrary, both from her own letters and from the writings of her relations, and to show how completely such a conclusion misrepresents her attitude of mind towards the highest questions. But all serious students of her biography may be left to discover this for themselves. They can weigh the assertions made in 'La Vie' against the testimony given by those who knew her intimately as to her faith, unselfishness, humility, and the 'piety which ruled her in

life and supported her in death.' Above
all, they will examine the records of that
closing scene, when face to face with a
comparatively early death, ' neither her love
of God nor her fellow creatures flagged for
a moment,' and will consider whether such
faith, courage, and entire submission to the
Divine will could have been felt by one to
whom religion was 'merely a matter of
externals.'

Mlle. Villard's book is, as a literary
criticism, so exhaustive and valuable that
it will probably be accepted in France as a
standard work on Jane Austen and her novels.
It may have already served to increase the
number of readers in that country, and this
number is likely to become larger, for at the
present time, when a strong desire is felt that
the bonds between our nearest Ally and ourselves should be drawn closer, those formed
by a mutual study of each other's literature
can hardly be neglected. As it must be
desirable that correct ideas of the writer of
any English classic should be offered to the
French nation, those who are the most nearly
concerned in seeing that justice is done to
the personal character of Jane Austen, and

who are best able to speak of it from authentic
and unimpeachable testimony, could hardly
be excused if they failed to offer a protest
against the estimate regarding it put forth
in 'La Vie,' as being utterly unworthy of her
and entirely misleading in respect of a vital
part of her nature. It is well to recall that
this was comprehended and rightly described
by a juster and more discriminating judge
nearly one hundred years ago, when Archbishop Whately, in the *Quarterly Review*, thus
summed up his estimate of herself and her
works [1]:

'Miss Austen introduces very little of
what is technically called religion into her
books, yet that must be a blinded soul which
does not recognise the vital essence, every-
where present in her pages, of a deep and
enlightened piety.'

[1] *Quarterly Review*, No. XXIV, January, 1821.

NOTE.—The present writer is happy to state that she
has received an assurance from Mlle. Villard that the misapprehensions relating to Jane Austen's character objected
to in this chapter shall be revised and amended in any
future edition of 'La Vie.'

H

CHAPTER VI

' LADY SUSAN '

WHEN ' Lady Susan ' first appeared in print,
this title being prefixed to the second
edition of Mr. Austen Leigh's original
' Memoir,' it was remarked by more than
one critic that so short a story should
hardly have been allowed to give a name
to a whole volume. With this observation
the editor entirely agreed. He knew it had
been arranged that the tale itself should be
placed after the ' Memoir,' together with other
unpublished writings of the author, and, therefore, when the second edition of his work
appeared, bearing the title of ' Lady Susan,'
he felt both surprise and regret. He foresaw
the disappointment of its readers when they
should discover the nature and brevity of
the story, and still more did he feel that to
put forward, as though on a par with her
other works, a character sketch which she

never intended to give to the world, would not appear on his own part to be showing due respect to the memory and judgment of his aunt. So scrupulous was he on this point that even in writing the short notice prepared for it, when he had no expectation that the title would be affixed to the whole volume, he said, 'If it should be judged unworthy of the publicity now given to it, the censure must fall on him who has put it forth and not on her who kept it locked up in her desk.'

The exact date of its composition is uncertain, but there are several reasons for preferring an early one. It was written in letters, the form used in some of the novels known to Jane Austen almost from childhood and employed by her when she was very young in (*a*) an unpublished fragment, (*b*) the first version of ' Sense and Sensibility, called ' Elinor and Marianne,' and again (*c*) in ' Lady Susan,' which seems to place the latter in the category of early compositions. This, it is true, would not be a sufficient proof if taken alone.   The author may have thought that the most forcible way of dealing with Lady Susan would be by leaving her

to speak for herself, and might therefore have
chosen to narrate the history in the form of
letters. Critics have observed, not unnatu-
rally, that this remarkable analysis of a
vicious woman's nature seems a strange
subject for a young girl either to have attempted or to have succeeded in, and such
a conviction has made it the more difficult for
them to imagine what date should be assigned
to the work. There is, we believe, but one
solution to this puzzle, one that was discerned
by a correspondent of the present writer,
whose position had enabled him to observe
human nature closely, and who, though
knowing Jane Austen's six novels well, had
recently read 'Lady Susan' for the first
time. He says in his letter concerning the
book, 'I find it very clever. It is, of course,
more bitter and worldly than her other
works, but it shows a tremendous insight
into shams. I feel quite sure the character
is drawn from life.' How far the last remark
is justified by facts may be decided after the
reader has perused the following true history
taken from a family MS.

'About two hundred years ago, Mr. and
Mrs. — —, well-connected people, were

living on their property in the Midlands,
with a family of one son and five daughters.
The daughters had but a rough life. Their
mother, a beautiful woman and most cour-
teous and fascinating in society, was of a
stern, tyrannical temper. They were brought
up in fear, not in love. They were sometimes
not allowed proper food, but were required
to eat what was loathsome to them, and were
often relieved from hunger by the maids
privately bringing them up bread and cheese
after they were in bed. Perhaps some of
the traditions of their mother's personal
cruelty to her children as endangering their
lives went beyond the truth, but there could
be no doubt that she was a very unkind and
severe mother. When making long visits
from home it was her custom to take one
daughter with her to act, it was said, as her
maid. On one occasion, all her daughters
being then young women, and one of them
being married, she did so—taking one daughter
with her, and leaving three at home. Her
absence lasted for several months. Their
father, so far as is known, was likewise
absent. Two of the three daughters took
this opportunity of marrying, but not in

their own condition of life. One married the son of a neighbouring yeoman, and the other, a friend of her new brother-in-law, a horse-dealer. The first marriage turned out not so very bad, but the second was deplorable. The remaining sister, knowing how much her mother would resent these mis-alliances, and foreseeing nothing but increased severity in the house, could not resolve to face her anger. She also left her home before Mrs. —— could get back to it. All the sisters had £500 a-piece, left to them by an uncle—and on the interest of this little sum she resolved to try and live.' The further history of the last daughter was brighter. Friends and relations assisted her, and she finally made a suitable marriage in her own rank in life. Mrs. ——, when afterwards left a widow, married a gentleman of good property, with whom she had long been well acquainted. The descendants of the last-named daughter always spoke of her as ' the cruel Mrs. ——.' Among these, Jane, as a young girl, had intimate friends, and the whole tale would naturally become known to her. That it was so is also shown by a passage in one of her letters, perfectly comprehensible to those who are acquainted with the names and details belonging to the foregoing history.

This being certain, and it being also certain that she wrote 'Lady Susan,' there is no room for doubt that the two facts are closely related to each other, and that she could not have depicted an inhuman, repulsive mother, carrying on her barbarities beneath a mask of charm and beauty, without having constantly before her thoughts the prototype of this exceptional character, of whose actual existence she was well aware. Why this knowledge caused her to write such a sketch—not for publication—may claim a moment's thought. To strongly imaginative and sensitive souls, 'wax to receive, and marble to retain,' revelations of beauty and glory, or of darkness and horror, come with a force beyond that which others can know, leaving an impression, amounting to a possession of the soul, not to be flung off until relief has been found through some outward and concrete act. When Byron died, and all the Tennyson family mourned him, it was Alfred who, as a boy, rushed out and endeavoured to express his sense of England's unspeakable loss by carving on a rock of sandstone, 'Byron

is dead.' He may have felt that in this way
he and nature could mourn together, and
that he had at least done something to record
the despair of his heart in the face of this
great calamity. A similar intensity of feeling,
though this time of horrified indignation, may
have seized upon Jane Austen's soul when
the story of an unnatural and brutal mother
was made known to her, overpowering her
fancy to so great a degree that she was at
last impelled to seek relief in gibbeting this
repulsive being by setting down her character
in writing, thus to express the depth of her
disgust through the medium of her own
peculiar Art.

So far as we know, it is the only ' Study
from Life ' that she ever made, nor was it
now accomplished in order that it might
appear again in any of her longer works.
She once said that ' it was her desire to create,
not to reproduce,' and there is nothing in the
novels which calls ' Lady Susan ' to mind,
unless some hint of her unblushing worldliness can be found in Mary Crawford's letter
to Fanny or of her maternal harshness in
Mrs. Ferrars' behaviour to her eldest son.
We are, therefore, compelled to believe that

the horror which oppressed her imagination, when reflecting on this picture of outward beauty and secret barbarity, could not be relieved without giving expression to her sense of its enormity by placing it upon paper. Had she never heard the tale, her youth might have saved her from conceiving the possibility of so evil a being, but having heard it, that same youth would intensify the repulsion and disgust it must create within her. That the sketch was not meant to meet the public eye is clear, partly because, in 1803, she attempted to publish a novel in two volumes, then called ' Susan,' later ' Catherine,' and finally ' Northanger Abbey,' and she would not have wished to give the same name to two published works, and yet more so because the strong resemblance between the character of ' Lady Susan ' and that of her friends' ancestress would render such a thought impossible to her scrupulous sense of honour. The structure of the story itself confirms this view. Incident and plot are neglected throughout its course, in which there is little attempt to elaborate any character in such a way as to arouse the interest of the reader. The book is a figure-piece, with a cruel, heartless woman for its single subject. In comparison with this central object, the rest of the *dramatis personæ* are but shadowy beings. Of one of these the author writes at the close that 'it must already have been evident that Mr. Vernon existed only to do whatever might be required of him,' and the same remark may be applied with a slight expansion in its meaning to the whole of the company, who exist merely to bring out the various vices united in one woman, a creature entirely devoid of conscience, and without a single redeeming quality.

That such unnatural mothers can be found is unhappily certain, a fact proved by the existence of a modern society for 'Prevention of Cruelty to Children'—generally from the cruelty of their own parents—but that they are on the whole rare is also happily true, and so great a monster is not to be met with anywhere in the six published novels. In this the author shows her usual wisdom. An artist, speaking of landscape painting, has observed that 'Nature employs only small spots of deep dark,' and the same may be said of that field of Nature in which

Jane Austen painted—human nature. She did not commit the mistake of taking exceptions for rules, nor of thinking the world must be villainous as a whole because some villains can be found in it. She avoids the use of ' deep darks,' and employs but seldom the lighter shades of evil, coarseness, and vulgarity, being, as it would seem, unwilling to blacken her canvas more than might be found necessary in order to provide some contrast to the brighter and purer tints of her picture. That she had either kind at command, should she choose to make use of them, is proved by the introduction, in their proper places, of Mr. Price and Nancy Steele, and, above all, by the more lately revealed character, ' Lady Susan,' who is drawn with an unsparing hand, showing that ' tremendous insight into shams ' already mentioned. This inborn gift must have been greatly quickened by hearing the history of Mrs. ——. It would teach her to look below the surface, even in the case of parents and children, and would serve to assure her, whenever in the future she was describing parental harshness or tyranny, that she was still keeping well within the mark.

Although 'Lady Susan' must be placed in a totally different category from the other novels, it should not be neglected by anyone who wishes to form a just estimate of Jane Austen's varied powers as a writer, or of herself as a woman. That she drew such a portrait once enlarges our conception of her genius; that she never drew such another increases our value for her as a woman. She chose wholesome, sane, cheerful subjects, 'things of good report,' for her own imagination and that of her readers to dwell upon, describing evil as little as possible and never with a needless detail. This consideration will, it is thought, give additional force to what has been already said respecting the silent strength of her moral character. We can thus learn how to appreciate the self-control with which she resists any temptation to the use of extravagant language in describing emotions and situations, such as has earned for later writers the title of 'intense,' deeming it to be beneath the dignity both of true art and of that which is highest and best in human nature.

The words of an American writer, Mr. W. L. Phelps, well deserve to be quoted here:

'Let no one believe,' he says, 'that Jane Austen's men and women are deficient in passion because they behave with decency; to those who have the power to see and interpret there is a depth of passion in her characters that far surpasses the emotional power displayed in many novels where the lovers seem to forget the meaning of such words as honour, virtue, and fidelity.' These words Jane Austen certainly never forgot, either as an author or a woman. Several passages in her personal history show her to have been possessed of keen sensibility and deep attachments, but we know that her own sensations never made her indifferent to the claims of those with whom she lived, nor caused her to forget the call of ' Self-reverence, self-honour, self-control.' Tennyson's words she could not know, but the spirit that inspired them was akin to her own. Neither is there any evidence that she was acquainted with Wordsworth's poems, though the earliest of these were published twenty-four years before her own death. She probably never saw ' Laodamia,' written three years prior to that event, but if Wordsworth knew her writings and had wished to give a voice to

her consistent utterances concerning the
strongest of all human emotions, he could
not have done so more fittingly than in
Protesiláus' well-known lines :

'Be taught, O faithful Consort, to control
Rebellious passion : for the Gods approve
The depth, and not the tumult, of the soul;
A fervent, not ungovernable, love.'

CHAPTER VII

PARENTS AND CHILDREN

MENTION has already been made of various mistaken rumours spread abroad concerning Jane Austen during the first half-century that followed her death, one of these being that 'she did not like children.' No supposition could have been further from the truth. On no point is the family testimony more unanimous than on the unfailing love and kindness she bestowed upon them, together with the warm love they felt for her in return. She was quickly provided with such objects of affection, as four of her five brothers had families, and two nieces were born before she was herself grown up, both of whom lived to become, as young women, her close and intimate friends. Another younger niece has written: ' My visits to Chawton were frequent. I cannot tell when they began. They were very pleasant to me and Aunt Jane was the great charm. As a very little girl I was always creeping up to her and following her whenever I could, in the house and out of it. Her charm to children was great sweetness of manner; she seemed to love you, and you loved her naturally in return. This was what I felt in my earliest days, before I was old enough to be amused by her cleverness. But soon came the delight of her playful talk. *Everything* she could make amusing to a child. Then, as I got older and cousins came to share the entertainment, she would tell us the most delightful stories, chiefly of Fairyland, and her Fairies had all characters of their own. The tale was invented, I am sure, on the spur of the moment, and was sometimes continued for two or three days if occasion served. I believe we were, all of us, according to our different ages and natures very fond of our Aunt Jane, and that we ever retain a strong impression of the pleasantness of Chawton life. One of my cousins, after he was grown up, used occasionally to go and see Aunt Cassandra, *then* left the sole inmate of the old house, and he told me that his visits were always a disappointment to him, for that he could not help expecting to feel

CHAWTON COTTAGE.

Jane Austen's House   Chawton M

particularly happy at Chawton, and never, till he got there, could he realise to himself how all its peculiar pleasures were gone.' Similar testimony on these points has been given by another niece—the little Anna who, when three years old, was placed by her widowed father, James Austen, at Steventon Rectory, to be ' mothered ' by his two sisters. Anna composed stories of her own long before she was old enough to write them down, and had always a vivid recollection of the way in which her kind Aunt Jane performed that office for her. On reaching the age of seven she dictated to her aunt a drama founded on ' Sir Charles Grandison,' which still exists in Jane Austen's handwriting. Anna's half brother and sister, Edward and Caroline, had the same love of inventing stories, and all brought their compositions to be read and reviewed by their Aunt Jane—Anna continuing the practice as a young woman when she had embarked on what was intended to be a serious novel. For an author to be ready at any time to put aside her own writings—and such writings —in order to interest herself in these very young performances shows that entire unselfishness of nature and ready sympathy with the wants of childhood which was always ascribed to Jane Austen by those who truly knew her.

Her pen was often at their service when they were apart, for she wrote them charming notes, with many playful turns, containing now and then a little good advice as well. Her niece Caroline has truly said that 'in addressing a child she was perfect.' She lived indeed in a circle of childhood, and when we look at her books we see how steady and consistent a place children take in them— without uttering a word ! The old-fashioned maxim that, when in company, children should always be seen and not heard, was no doubt one on which Jane had herself been brought up, and she observes the same rule as regards the children of her fancy ; the reader is not troubled with any of their remarks. Even the elder among them are not allowed to say much. The author advised her niece Anna to remember that, in novel writing, ' girls are not interesting until they are grown up,' consequently of the speeches of little Fanny Price and her cousins only enough are given to show in few words

their relative conditions and characters, to
bring out the kindness of Edmund and the
negligence of his sisters. Margaret Dashwood,
as a half-grown girl, utters a few remarks
equally malàpropos in themselves, and àpropos
to the conduct of the story. But the younger
ones are all silent, yet not the less valuable
on that account. They provide motives for
action and conversation on the part of their
elders, and are even allowed on one occasion
to take a small share in carrying on the drama
of the plot. No fewer than twenty children,
known to us by number or by name, and
generally by the latter, appear in the course
of the six novels, without counting the vaguer
groups of little Harvilles at Lyme, and happily
occupied little Perrys at Highbury. However
slight the sketch may be, we can always
recognise in it the sure touch of one who
herself moved about childhood's realm as a
constant visitor and a ready sympathiser.
If we try to imagine Jane Austen's novels
deprived of their children, we shall see that
in some cases they could hardly be carried on
at all, while in every instance that sense of
simple truthfulness, of warmth, and of life
which they now possess would be greatly

lessened or altogether wanting. Just as in the figure-pieces of early Italian masters the charm is enhanced and the general effect is completed by those miniature hills, rivers, and houses in the background, which provide a fitting setting for the central objects upon which they are never suffered unduly to intrude, so do Jane Austen's little people fill up, furnish, and decorate in a suitable manner the more distant portions of her scenes. Though at no time allowed to put themselves forward, they are, in their proper places and angles, highly useful by imparting a constant feeling of reality and by supplying a due sense of perspective, atmosphere, colouring, and space.

What is there, then, to be found in these books that could have led anyone to suppose their author did not like children ? The idea must have rested on the fact that she did not like spoilt children, or, rather, that she strongly objected to the spoiling of children—a subject on which it is evident she bestowed a good deal of thought. But that this showed no want of interest in the children themselves may be read in a letter, written towards the close of her life to a niece, after she had been spending some days in a house filled with younger cousins of the latter. She says: 'Though the children are sometimes very noisy and not under such order as they ought and easily might [be], I cannot help liking them or even loving them, which I hope may be not wholly inexcusable in their, and your, affectionate Aunt Jane Austen.' Here we see at once, not only a natural quickness of vision towards children, but also the even balance of her judgment when reviewing the whole case, 'the children might, and should [have been] kept in better order.'

It was towards the middle of the last century that a striking tale appeared, named 'A School for Fathers,' in which a charming young hero is forced into a duel, against his own inclination, by parental pride, and falls in consequence fatally wounded. Jane Austen's novels may be not unjustly entitled 'A School for Parents,' and this not merely with reference to the young children to be found in them, who are over-indulged by mothers until they become an annoyance to everyone. Her outlook goes much further than this. Our language, unfortunately, contains no word expressive of the connection between parents and their sons and daughters, after the latter have ceased to be ' children '— properly speaking—and are becoming, or have become, men and women. But it is in these later stages of life that we find Jane Austen exhibiting to us the results of early training or of its absence. We do not learn this only in the case of such spoilt children as the little Middletons and Betsy Price, for older examples are as plainly dealt with, and their parents' faults are indicated with equal clearness. Mr. Allen, who is ' a sensible man,' soon discovers that ' Mrs. Thorpe is, without doubt, too indulgent to her daughters,' and we have Isabella in consequence. Mrs. Dashwood tells Marianne to ascribe her misfortunes to ' her mother's imprudence,' a remark with which the reader will easily agree — while of Mrs. Bennet it is enough to say that she was exactly fitted to be the mother of Lydia. Irreproachable parents—mothers especially—are indeed greatly in the way of any novelist, who has to get them out of the way as handsomely as may be. This truth was discerned very early in her own literary career by Jane Austen, one of her

girlish fragments, called ' Kitty, or The Bower,'
beginning with these words : ' Kitty ' (afterwards changed to Catherine) ' had the mis-
fortune, as many heroines have had before her,
of losing both her parents while she was still
quite young.' But even when the maternal
parent has been disposed of by death or by
distance, the daughter must, none the less,
be brought up or brought out by someone,
who may contrive to go as far wrong in the
process as any mother herself could do. Mrs.
Weston, charming and sensible though she
was, had been ruled for many years by her
own charge, Emma ; Edmund and Fanny
agree in ascribing Mary Crawford's want of
principle to deficiencies in the education she
had received from her aunt, together with
the bad example set by her uncle ; and the
one error into which Anne Elliot falls is
spoken of as having been due to the mistaken
advice of an older friend, who has over her
almost the influence of a mother. Nor are
the fathers spared. Mrs. Ferrars is the only
instance of unfeeling harshness among the
mothers, while both General Tilney and Sir
Walter Elliot are absolutely unpardonable
fathers, and there is also a good deal requiring

forgiveness in Mr. Woodhouse, Sir Thomas Bertram, and—not least—in Mr. Bennet, one of the author's most surprising creations. She had, as we have seen, gained a knowledge when still quite young, through a history belonging to past days, of the depths to which parental cruelty can descend, and we have also seen how this knowledge very probably quickened her insight respecting lighter shades of the same evil visible around her, the evil, it may be, 'that is wrought from want of thought, and not from want of heart.' Shortcomings on the side of parents are not shown to us merely by Jane Austen herself, speaking from her position as author, since she frequently points out that they were clearly apprehended by a daughter of their own. Some time later, a school of fiction arose, intended to a great extent for the young, in which it would have been held highly disrespectful for daughters to comment adversely, even to themselves, upon any action on the part of their parents, while to utter a remonstrance to either father or mother on their neglect of a parent's duties, would have been looked upon as an unpardonable liberty. Jane Austen, however, takes a different view, and never blames her

heroines for possessing some acquaintance
with the characters of those by whom they
had been brought up, being, as it would seem,
of opinion that they could not become rational
and thinking beings without acquiring such
a perception, which she has no hesitation in
attributing to some of the best among them.
Poor Eleanor Tilney, when compelled to turn
Catherine Morland out of the house, can only
exclaim, ' Alas ! for my feelings as a daughter.
He is certainly greatly, very greatly, discom-
posed. I have seldom seen him more so.'
Anne Elliot, who ' often wished her knowledge of her father's character were less,'
could not but be aware of the weak vanity
that laid him open to Mrs. Clay's insidious
designs, while the most striking example of
filial insight and resolution in character in
all the novels is to be found in Elizabeth
Bennet's remonstrance with her father on his
neglect of responsibility as a parent. It must
have been a hard task, but when it was over
she ' felt confident of having performed her
duty,' a reflection that can only do her
honour in the mind of the reader, and,
coupled with Mr. Bennet's most characteristic
reference to it after Lydia's elopement had

taken place, shows that it had done her honour in his judgment also. Though distrust of a parent's wisdom was the compelling cause of the action taken both by Elizabeth and by Anne, there was no lack of filial respect in their manner of performing it. This is at no time wanting on the part of her heroines, even towards those for whom it was impossible that love should be felt. Where this did exist, parental shortcomings were never suffered to check it. Marianne Dashwood ardently loved her mother, imprudent though she had shown herself to be, and Emma Woodhouse, when engaged to the man of her heart, at once formed a solemn resolution never to quit her father, and ' even wept over the idea of it, as a sin of thought.'

We must, then, come to the conclusion that Jane Austen's quick intuition had deeply impressed upon her the extreme importance of parental duties being well performed and of the evils sure to follow if these were neglected. Dogmatic she never was, but her own light and delicate touches, joined to the working out of various incidents in her plots, sufficiently indicate the views she held on this point and give us some cause to suspect that, if things went wrong between the two parties, her sympathies would be mostly found on the side of the children, even when over-indulged and, consequently, troublesome. For these she was unwilling to abandon hope, and here Mr. Knightley is deputed to speak her mind. When Emma looks forward to Mrs. Weston's educating her infant daughter in a perfect manner, since she had had the advantage of practising first upon herself—'That is,' replied Mr. Knightley, 'she will indulge her even more than she did you, and believe that she does not indulge her at all. It will be the only difference.'

'Poor child!' cried Emma, 'at that rate what will become of her?'

'Nothing very bad—the fate of thousands. She will be disagreeable in infancy and correct herself as she grows older. I am losing all my bitterness against spoilt children, my dearest Emma. I, who am owing all my happiness to *you*, would it not be horrible ingratitude in me to be severe on them?'

Jane Austen could also admit the existence of other influences likely to affect the ultimate fate of children. She could take

into consideration the child's own character
and the power of surrounding circumstances.
The young Prices, not through parental good
training, but in spite of its absence, prospered
when aided by Sir Thomas Bertram, on
account of ' The advantages of early hardships
and discipline,' and ' The consciousness of
being born to struggle and endure.' Such a
consciousness, meeting with a like success,
their efforts being in this instance encouraged
by their own parents, Jane may have often
rejoiced over when reflecting upon the
careers of her two sailor brothers.

' Persuasion ' supplies us with a very
different type of sailor, whose ill-doing is
ascribed to his own perverse character and
not to any neglect on the part of his parents.
Many readers have objected to the terms in
which the unlucky Dick Musgrove's history
and his mother's lamentations over him are
described ; they have been thought hard
and unworthy of Jane Austen's kind heart
and delicate taste. One reply alone can be
made to this charge. Though she wrote this
passage, she did not publish it. On March
13, 1817, four months before her own death,
she tells her niece, Fanny Knight, ' I have a

something ready for publication, which may perhaps come out in a twelve months time.' And again on March 23, 'Do not be surprised at finding Uncle Henry acquainted with my having another ready for publication. I could not say No when he asked me, but he knows nothing more of it. You will not like it, so you need not be impatient. You will, perhaps, like the heroine, as she is almost too good for me.' Why Fanny was not to like it does not appear, but the tone of these remarks, coupled with the author's intention of keeping it laid by for a whole year, points clearly in the direction of an intended revision when a considerable length of time should have elapsed. Her brother Henry's testimony confirms the belief that such was her usual custom. He says : 'Though in composition she was equally rapid and correct, yet an invincible distrust of her own judgment induced her to withhold her works from the public till time and many perusals had satisfied her that the charm of recent composition was dissolved.' A possible allusion to this practice may be found in the advice she offered to her niece Anna, when the latter was composing a novel: 'I hope when you

have written a great deal more you will feel
equal to scratching out some of the past.'

The book, though called 'ready for publication,' in the sense, perhaps, that its final
page had been written, does not seem to
have been ready for perusal, nor as yet
for announcement to her frequent confidant,
Henry, to whom, even after his persistent
enquiries had forced her to confess its existence,
it was not to be shown at present. In another
way it was certainly unfinished; it had
received no name. Younger generations of
the family learnt subsequently, through their
Aunt Cassandra, that this question had been
a good deal discussed between Jane and
herself, and that among several possible
titles, the one that seemed most likely to be
chosen was 'The Elliots.' Nothing, however, was finally settled, and Henry Austen,
to whose care it had been bequeathed,
brought it out under the name of 'Persuasion,'
re-naming at the same time her other work
left in MS. which she had called 'Catherine,'
but which he published as 'Northanger
Abbey.' Though it is possible to object to
both titles, as overweighting either book
by referring to one incident or one division,
rather than to the entire work, criticism

must give way to thankfulness that we possess them, even in a slightly imperfect condition, and what the fate of one might have been had its author lived longer is rendered a little questionable by her words to Fanny Knight in March, 1817: 'Miss Catherine is put upon the shelf for the present, and I do not know that she will ever come out.' Had she never done so, much delight must have been lost to many readers, and not a few streets and terraces in Bath would have been the poorer in associations for all those who now love to imagine they are treading in the steps of Morlands, Thorpes, and Tilneys, while 'Persuasion' has so captured some hearts that their owners feel inclined to assign to it the highest place of all. Nevertheless, when judgment is passed upon the position that Jane Austen's books have won as English classics, it should be remembered that 'Emma' is the last novel put forth by her as a completely finished work of art ; while it is open to anyone to believe that changes might, and probably would, have been made in her later and unpublished story had she herself survived to the close of the twelve months which she had allotted to it as a term of silent retirement.

There is still one theory, advanced by a reviewer, that must be mentioned before quitting the subject dealt with in this chapter, as it concerns Jane Austen's personal experience of the relations subsisting between parents and children. He takes up a position that these, in Steventon Rectory, were not pleasant, and that the family circle did not contain enough union and sympathy among its members for Jane to have felt or witnessed much domestic happiness beneath her father's roof, and that on this account she hardly ever gives in her books any description of a happy and affectionate family party. A most extraordinary theory indeed! It leads us to enquire how far its inventor has closely studied either her books or her biographies. Did he altogether forget Mrs. Dashwood and her daughters—their grief at parting and their eagerness for a reunion? Or the household of the John Knightleys, with its master's 'strong domestic habits and all sufficiency of home to himself'? Or the return of Catherine Morland to Fullerton, where, in spite of her woes as a heroine, she was welcomed with such affectionate eagerness that ' in the embrace of each she

found herself soothed, surrounded, caressed—
even happy ' ?   Or the Crofts—never satisfied
if apart—or the Westons, the Harvilles in
quitting whose house ' Anne thought she
left great happiness behind her '—or the
Gardiners, and the ' fine family piece ' of
the Christmas party at Uppercross, alive with
boys and girls, Mr. Musgrove with children
clamouring on his knees and Mrs. Musgrove
glancing happily round the room and observing
that ' After all she had gone through nothing
was so likely to do her good as a little quiet
cheerfulness at home ' ?

Whether we examine her writings or her
memoirs we are equally led to believe that no
one knew better than Jane Austen, both by
observation and experience, the meaning of
the word ' home ' in its fullest and best sense.
So baseless is the conjecture mentioned above
that we may rather say the conditions of life
to be found in her father's house would
quicken her perception of the contrast afforded
to them by some other families, through an
absence of peace and harmony in the latter
between parents and children, brothers and
sisters.   To assume that these were lacking
in Steventon Rectory is a most unwarrant-
able conclusion, and one that is absolutely

opposed to the truth. Evidence on this point is, happily, equally abundant and convincing. Mrs. George Austen, writing in 1796 to Mary Lloyd, soon to become her daughter-in-law, speaks of her own and her husband's heartfelt satisfaction in the prospect of ' adding you to the number of our very good children.' In a letter written more than twenty years later she explains to her sister-in-law, Mrs. Leigh Perrot, the particulars of her income, and dwells upon the eagerness all her sons had shown, when she had been left a widow in 1805, to make it a comfortable one. Of her two eldest she says : ' Mr. Knight (the second son) has a most active mind, a clear head, and a sound judgment ; he is quite a man of business. That my dear James was not. Classical knowledge, literary taste, and the power of elegant composition he possessed in the highest degree. To these Mr. Knight makes no pretensions. *Both* equally good, amiable, and sweet-tempered.'

The feelings and the conduct of all her sons on the death of their father are shown in letters written to the one then absent on naval duty (Captain Frank Austen) by his brothers at home. Henry laments the

loss of ' the best of Fathers and of Men,'
adding ' Language is so inadequate to what
we all feel on such a subject that you will
know why I prefer silence to imperfect
praise. The survivors are now what we
must all think of.' The letters that then
passed between the brothers on the question
of making a comfortable provision for their
mother are equally remarkable for the
generosity they display towards herself and
for the courtesy and affection they exhibit
towards each other. When the result was
finally made known to Mrs. Austen she
exclaimed that ' Never were children so
good as hers,' at the same time declining
to accept the whole of the income which
they offered her.

The author of the original ' Memoir '
has indicated that if there were a family
fault, it lay in exactly the opposite direction
from that suggested by this critic. He says :
' There was so much that was agreeable in this
family party that its members may be excused if they were inclined to live somewhat
too exclusively within it. They might see
in each other much to love and esteem
and something to admire.' To this may be
added, from family tradition, that of all the

party, Jane was the one chiefly conscious of this family tendency, and most alive to the duty of struggling against it. To this another testimony may be added, that of the last-named writer's sister, Caroline Austen, who, as a child and young girl, was often at Chawton Cottage both before and after her Aunt Jane's death; nor could any more fitting words be found than hers with which to close these 'Personal Aspects of Jane Austen.' 'In the time of my childhood, it was a cheerful house, my uncles, one or another, frequently coming for a few days, and they were all pleasant in their own families; I have thought since, after seeing more of other households, *wonderfully* so. The family talk had much spirit and vivacity, and it was never troubled by disagreement, as it was not their habit to argue with one another. There was always perfect harmony amongst the brothers and sisters, with firm family union, never broken but by death, and over my Grandmother's door might have been inscribed the text:

' Behold how good and joyful a thing it is,
Brethren, to dwell together in unity.'

APPENDIX

Some additional information respecting Jane Austen and the family party immediately surrounding her may be acceptable to that inner circle of her readers who are willing to bear with a little repetition of facts in order to glean, from original documents, a few particulars not yet fully known to them. It is to such readers that the following extracts and remarks are offered.

The original 'Memoir,' after giving the account of her funeral, closes with these words : ' Her brothers went back sorrowing to their several homes. They were very fond and very proud of her . . . and each loved afterwards to fancy a resemblance in some niece or daughter of his own to the dear sister Jane, whose perfect equal they yet never expected to see.' Of these nieces, many were at that time so young that such a resemblance could develop at a later period only. The three of whom she had seen most were, Fanny Knight, her brother Edward's eldest daughter; Anna Austen, her brother James's eldest daughter, who, prior to her Aunt Jane's death, had married Benjamin Lefroy of Ashe (son of Madam Lefroy, Jane Austen's beloved friend); and Anna's half-sister Caroline Austen. It was of the latter that their father wrote in April, 1819: 'Caroline has that playfulness of mind, united with an affectionate heart, which so peculiarly marked our lamented Jane.' Fatherly partiality did not mislead him in his high estimate of this daughter. Like her Aunt Jane, she had gifts both of humour and pathos, which, combined with a similar originality and independence of mind, made her in later years a delightful companion and a charming converser. Like her, also, she, in her turn, became a perfect aunt to whom nephews and nieces are indebted for many kindnesses, one of these being the manner in which she related, both by word of mouth and in writing, family history and personal reminiscences. One of these gives an account of her elder

sister's wedding.[1] This event was deeply
interesting to her grandmother, Mrs. Austen,
and to her aunts, Cassandra and Jane, the
first-named sending good wishes to the bride,
both in prose and verse. Nevertheless, all
three stayed quietly at home, making no
attempt to attend the ceremony, though
Steventon and Chawton are but sixteen miles
apart. It is true that sixteen miles of indifferent road then formed a considerable
barrier in wintry weather for ladies who
possessed no carriage and horses, but their
absence from the wedding is a fresh proof
of the customary simplicity of procedure on
these occasions, such as we meet with in
'Mansfield Park' and in 'Emma,' which
strongly characterised Anna Austen's wedding day.

Caroline Austen writes: 'On the 8th
November, 1814, my sister was married to
Benjamin Lefroy, Esq. He had not then
taken orders, although of the full age that
was necessary. Weddings were then usually
very quiet. The old fashion of festivity
and publicity had quite gone by, and was

[1] Published by permission in Miss Hill's book, *Jane
Austen's Homes and Friends.*

universally condemned as showing the bad
taste of former generations. But it revived
again, and no protest is now ever heard
against it. My Sister's wedding was certainly in the extreme of quietness; yet
not so as to be in any way remarked upon,
or censured, and this was the order of the
day: The Bridegroom came from Ashe
Rectory, where he had hitherto lived with
his Brother; and Mr. and Mrs. Lefroy (his
Brother and Sister-in-law) came with him,
as well as another brother, Mr. Edward
Lefroy. Anne Lefroy, the eldest little girl,
was one of the Bridemaids and I was the
other. My Brother came from Winchester
that morning, but was to stay only a few
hours. We in the house had a slight early
breakfast upstairs; and between nine and
ten the Bride, my Mother, Mrs. Lefroy, Anne
and myself, were taken to Church in our
carriage; all the gentlemen walked. The
weather was dull and cloudy but it did not
actually rain. The season of the year, the
unfrequented road of half a mile to the lonely
old Church, the grey light within of a
November morning, making its way through
the narrow windows, no stove to give warmth,
no flowers to give colour and brightness, no

friends, high or low, to offer their good wishes —
and so to claim some interest in the great
event of the day—all these circumstances
and deficiencies must, I think, have given a
gloomy air to our Wedding. Mr. Lefroy
read the service. My father gave his daughter
away. The Clerk, of course, was there, though
I do not particularly remember him, but I
am quite sure there was no one else in the
Church. Nor was anyone asked to the
Breakfast, to which we sat down as soon as
we got back. I do not think this idea of
sadness struck me at the time. The bustle
in the house and all the preparations had
excited me, and it seemed to me a festivity
from beginning to end.

' The Breakfast was such as best Breakfasts
then were. Some variety of bread, hot rolls,
buttered toast, tongue or ham, and eggs.
The addition of Chocolate at one end of the
table and the Wedding Cake in the middle
marked the speciality of the day. I and
Anne Lefroy, nine and six years old, wore
white frocks and had white ribband on our
straw bonnets, which I suppose were new
for the occasion. Soon after breakfast the
Bride and Bridegroom departed. They had
a long day's journey before them to Hendon.

The other Lefroys went home, and in the afternoon my Mother and I went to Chawton, to stay at the Great House, then occupied by my Uncle Captain (Francis) Austen and his large family. My Father stayed behind for a few days and then joined us. The servants had cake and wine in the evening, and Mr. Digweed walked down to keep my father company. Such were the Wedding festivities of Steventon in 1814 ! '

The dress of the bride has been recorded by one of her own daughters. ' She wore a dress of fine white muslin, and over it a soft silk shawl, white, shot with primrose, with embossed white satin flowers and very handsome fringe, and on her head a small cap to match, trimmed with lace, and the delicate yellow tints must have been most becoming to her bright brown hair, hazel eyes, and sunny, clear complexion.' The bride was then twenty-one, and was considered to be the prettiest girl in the neighbourhood, the most striking feature of her face being the widely-opened large dark eyes, which retained their brilliant beauty to the close of a long life. It was necessary for the bridal pair to start early that Bagshot

Heath, a resort of highwaymen, should be passed over in daylight. Jane Austen went up to her brother Henry's house in London a few days later, and had then the satisfaction of driving out to Hendon to visit her niece as a bride.[1] Anna and her husband afterwards returned from Hampstead to live in a house called ' Wyards,' within a walk of Chawton Village, and frequent communication with her relations in that place could thus be easily maintained.

CAROLINE AUSTEN ON THE LIFE AT CHAWTON
COTTAGE
Written in 1867

' I have been told the house had formerly been an Inn, and it was well placed for such a purpose, just where the road from Winchester comes into the London and Gosport road. The front door opened on the road ; a very narrow enclosure on each side protected the house from possible shock of any runaway vehicle. A good-sized entrance and two parlours, called dining and drawing-room, made up the length of the house, all intended originally to look on the road, but the large

[1] Cf. *Life and Letters*, Chap. XIX, p. 361.

drawing-room window was blocked up and
turned into a bookcase when Mrs. Austen
took possession, and another was opened at
the side which gave to view only turf and
trees. A high wooden fence shut out the
road (to Winchester) all the length of the
little domain, and trees were planted inside
to form a shrubbery walk which, carried
round the enclosure, gave a very sufficient
space for exercise. You did not feel cramped
for room, and there was a pleasant irregular
mixture of hedgerow and grass and gravel
walk, and long grass for mowing, and
Orchard, which I imagine arose from two
or three little enclosures having been thrown
together and arranged as best might be for
ladies' occupation. There was, besides, a good
kitchen garden ; large and many out buildings,
not much occupied. All this affluence of
space was very delightful to children, and I
have no doubt added considerably to the
pleasure of a visit. Everything, indoors
and out, was well kept, the house was well
furnished, and it was altogether a comfortable
and ladylike establishment, though I believe
the means which supported it were but small.
The house was quite as good as the generality

of Parsonage Houses then were, and much in the same old style, the ceilings low and roughly finished, some bedrooms very small, none very large, but in number sufficient to accommodate the inmates and several guests. The dining-room could not be made to look anywhere but on the road, and there my Grandmother often sat for an hour or two in the morning, with her work or her writing, cheered by its sunny aspect and by the stirring scene it afforded. I believe the close vicinity of the road was no more an evil to her than it was to her grandchildren. Collyer's daily coach with six horses was a sight to see!—and most delightful was it to a child to have the awful stillness of night frequently broken by the noise of passing carriages, which seemed sometimes even to shake the bed. The village of Chawton has, of course, long since been tranquillised; it is no more a great thoroughfare. . . . As to my Aunt Jane's personal appearance, hers was the first face that I can remember thinking pretty, not that I used that word to myself, but I know I looked at her with admiration. Her face was rather round than long; she had a bright, but not a pink, colour, a clear, brown complexion, and very good hazel eyes. She was not, I believe, an absolute beauty, but before she left Steventon she was established as a very pretty girl in the opinion of most of her neighbours, as I learnt afterwards from some of those who still remained. Her hair, a darkish brown, curled naturally in short curls round her face (for then ringlets were not). She always wore a cap. Such was the custom with ladies who were not quite young—at least of a morning—but I never saw her without one. My Aunts were particularly neat ; they held all untidy ways in great dis-esteem. Aunt Jane began the day with music, for which I conclude she had a natural taste, as she thus kept it up, though she had no one to teach, and was never induced (as I have heard) to play in Company, and none of her family cared much for it. I suppose that she might not trouble them she chose her practising time before breakfast, when she could have the room to herself. She practised regularly every morning. She played very pretty tunes, I thought, and I liked to stand by her and listen to her. Much that she played was from Manuscript copies written out by herself. . . .

At 9 o'clock she made breakfast—that was her part of the household work. The tea and sugar stores were under her charge—and the wine. Aunt Cassandra did all the rest, for my Grandmother had suffered herself to be superseded by her daughters *before* I can remember, and soon *after* she ceased even to sit at the head of the table.

'I don't believe Aunt Jane observed any particular method in parcelling out her day, but I think she generally sat in the drawing-room till luncheon, when visitors were there, chiefly at work. She was fond of work, and was a great adept at overcast and satin-stitch—the peculiar delight of that day. She was wonderfully successful with cup and ball, and found a resource sometimes in that simple game when she was suffering from weak eyes and could not work or read for long together. After luncheon my Aunts generally walked out ; sometimes they went to Alton for shopping, often, one or the other of them to the " Great House," as it was then called, in order, when a brother was inhabiting it, to make a visit ; or, if the house were standing empty, they liked to stroll about the grounds, sometimes to Chawton Park, a noble beech

wood, just within a walk, and sometimes—
but that was rarely—to call on a neighbour.
They had no carriage and their visitings did
not extend far. There were a few families
living in the village, but no great intimacy
was kept up with any of them ; they were on
friendly, but rather distant, terms with all.
Yet I am sure my Aunt Jane had a regard
for her neighbours, and felt a kindly interest
in their proceedings. She liked immensely
to hear all about them. They sometimes
served for her amusement, but it was her
own nonsense that gave zest to the gossip.
She never turned *them* into ridicule ; she was
as far as possible from being censorious or
satirical; she never abused them or " quizzed "
them. That was the word of the day—an
ugly one, now obsolete—and the ugly practice
which it bespoke is far less prevalent now,
under any name, than it was then. The
laugh she occasionally raised was by imagining
for her neighbours impossible contingencies, by
relating in prose or verse some trifling incident,
coloured to her own fancy, or in writing a
history of what they had said or done, that
could deceive nobody. My Aunt must have
spent much time in writing. Her desk lived

in the drawing-room ; I often saw her writing letters on it, and I believe she wrote much of her novels in the same way, sitting with her family when they were quite alone, but I never saw any manuscript of that sort in progress ' (Caroline may, however, have done so without knowing it, as it was her Aunt's habit to write them on note paper, the better to be able to cover them with blotting paper if a visitor were shown in). ' She wrote very fully to her brothers when they were at sea, and she corresponded with many others of the family. There is nothing in these letters which *I* have seen that would be acceptable to the public.   They were very well expressed, and they must have been very interesting to those who received them, but they detailed chiefly home and family events and she seldom committed herself even to any opinion, so that to strangers there could be no transcript of her mind ; they would not feel that they knew her any the better for having read them. They were rather overcautious for excellence. Her letters to Aunt Cassandra were, I daresay, open and confidential.   My Aunt looked them over and burnt the greater part as she told me three or four years before her own death.

L

She left or gave some as legacies to the nieces, but of those that I have seen several had portions cut out.' (The ' Brabourne letters ' did not appear during this writer's life-time.) ' When staying at Chawton, if my two cousins, Mary Jane and Cassy Austen, were there, we often had amusements in which my Aunt was very helpful. She was the one to whom we always looked for help. She would furnish us with what we wanted from her wardrobe and she would often be the entertaining visitor in our make-believe house. She amused us in various ways, once, I remember, in giving a conversation, as between myself and my two cousins, supposed to be grown up, the day after a ball. She was considered to read aloud remarkably well. I did not often hear her, but once I knew her take up a volume of Evelina and read a few pages of "Mr. Smith and the Branghtons," and I thought it was like a play. She had a very good speaking voice. This was the opinion of her contemporaries and though I did not *then* think of it as a perfection, or even hear it observed upon, yet its tones have never been forgotten. I can recall them even now, and I know they *were* very pleasant. Aunt Jane was a very affectionate sister to all her brothers. One of them in particular (Henry) was her especial pride and delight, but of all her family her nearest and dearest throughout her whole life was her only sister, Cassandra. Aunt Cassandra was the elder by three or four years, and the habit of looking up to her, begun in childhood, seemed always to continue. When I was a little girl, Aunt Jane would frequently say to me, if opportunity offered, that Aunt Cassandra could teach everything much better than she could—Aunt Cassandra knew more— Aunt Cassandra could tell me better whatever I wanted to know—all of which I received in respectful silence. Perhaps she thought my mind wanted a bias in that direction, but I truly believe that she did always really think of her sister as the superior to herself. . . . The most perfect confidence and affection ever subsisted between them, and great and lasting was the sorrow of the survivor when the final separation was made.'

The testimony given by Caroline's elder sister Anna is entirely to the same effect. ' Aunt Cassandra's loss in her sister was great indeed, and most truly a loss never to be repaired. They were everything to each other. They seemed to lead a life to themselves within the general family life which was shared only by each other. I will not say their true, but their *full*, feelings and opinions were known only to themselves. They alone fully understood what each had suffered and felt and thought. Yet they had such a gift of reticence that the secrets of their respective friends were never betrayed to each other. They were thoroughly trustworthy, and the young niece who brought her troubles to Aunt Jane for advice and sympathy knew she could depend absolutely on her silence, even to her sister.'

When writing to her brother, Capt. Frank Austen, then stationed in the Baltic, September, 1813, Jane refers to the fact of her authorship of 'Sense and Sensibility' and 'Pride and Prejudice' having been revealed by their brother Henry, and says: 'I know it is all done from affection and partiality, but at the same time let me here again express to you and Mary my sense of the *superior* kindness which you have shown on the occasion in doing what I wished. I am trying to harden myself. After all, what a trifle it is, in all its bearings, to the really important points of one's existence—even in this world.' She must have had an equally keen sense of gratitude to her eldest brother James and his wife (another Mary) for the strictly honourable silence they had preserved on the subject, in spite of what must have been a strong temptation to act otherwise. Their son Edward, then a boy at Winchester, had read both these books with great delight, but had never been told that his Aunt Jane had written them. Now, however, further silence was needless, and he has left a record of his feelings, on hearing the great news, in the following lines. Though written by a boy not yet quite fifteen years old, they are worth reading, if only to show the happy and intimate terms on which he and his Aunt Jane stood towards each other:—

To Miss J. Austen

'No words can express, my dear Aunt, my
    surprise
  Or make you conceive how I opened my
    eyes,

Like a pig Butcher Pile has just struck with
his knife,
When I heard for the very first time in my
life
That I had the honour to have a relation
Whose works were dispersed through the
whole of the nation.
I assure you, however, I'm terribly glad ;
Oh dear ! just to think (and the thought
drives me mad)
That dear Mrs. Jennings's good-natured
strain
Was really the produce of your witty brain,
That you made the Middletons, Dashwoods,
and all,
And that you (not young Ferrars) found out
that a ball
May be given in cottages, never so small.
And though Mr. Collins, so grateful for all,
Will Lady de Bourgh his dear Patroness
call,
'Tis to your ingenuity really he owed
His living, his wife, and his humble abode.
Now if you will take your poor nephew's
advice,
Your works to Sir William pray send in a
trice,

If he'll undertake to some grandees to show
    it,
By whose means at last the Prince Regent
    might know it,
For I'm sure if he did, in reward for your
    tale,
He'd make you a countess at least, without
    fail,
And indeed if the Princess should lose her
    dear life
You might have a good chance of becoming
    his wife.'

———

' Oh ! Journal. Oh ! Journal,
    Thou torment diurnal,
No Hydra so hopeless to slay !
    I demolish one head,
    Before going to bed,
And another starts up the next day ! '
MS.

These lines, composed about ninety years
ago, recurred involuntarily to the mind of
the present writer before this book was
finished. One reason for undertaking the
work was a desire to put an end if possible
to various misstatements made by com-

mentators respecting Jane Austen and her surroundings. To members of her own family some of these mistakes seem hardly excusable, but in the conviction that they were not ' set down in malice,' but only in haste, or in an unconscious desire to support some pre-conceived theory, it was hoped that by drawing together in a connected whole a variety of facts scattered throughout Jane Austen's biographies, all serious misrepresentations of her home, her family, and her own nature would be avoided in the future. But quite suddenly a new and strange tale respecting her has started up. It appears in an interesting book,[1] recently published, and as it may be widely read such a story cannot be left unnoticed. Miss Ethel Smyth, the authoress, who had a bachelor great uncle, Wm. Smyth, Master of Peterhouse, Cambridge, says : ' My father used to tell an odd little story about his uncle and Jane Austen, who were close friends. It appears that the authoress, wishing to get at his real opinion of one of her novels, put on a friend to pump him, concealing herself meanwhile behind a curtain. The

---

[1] *Impressions that Remained*, by Ethel Smyth, Mus. Doc. (Longmans & Co.)

verdict was luckily all that could be desired till the Professor remarked he was not quite certain as to her orthodoxy, having detected slight Unitarian leanings in her later works, upon which Jane Austen burst forth from her hiding place, indignantly crying: "That's not true!" One may question whether any degree of intimacy condones such a stratagem, but no doubt she knew her man.' Miss Smyth describes this as 'a curious sidelight on an elusive personality.'

For more than one reason this story cannot be accepted as accurate. That Dr. Smyth should discover in either of her 'later works,' 'Mansfield Park' and 'Emma,' Unitarian leanings, may surprise us, but it would be far more surprising could we believe that Jane Austen, with her high sense of honour, had chosen to imitate some of her own least worthy characters, the two Miss Steeles, by concealing herself in order to overhear anything concerning herself which she believed the speaker would have desired she should not hear. Elinor Dashwood's displeasure when she finds that Nancy Steele has been behaving in this way, cannot be forgotten by the readers of 'Sense and Sensibility.' Dr. Smyth may have been well acquainted with Jane Austen, though, as his name never appears in any extant letters, it must be uncertain whether he could have been ' a close friend ' of one who did not easily make such friends. But however well she may have known him, nothing would in her eyes have excused such conduct, nor will the hasty action and language here imputed to her appear, to those who have studied her books and her character, to bear any resemblance to her own. There are also other reasons for declining to accept the story as it now stands. ' Emma ' was published in December, 1815, and in the same month Jane Austen returned from London to her home at Chawton, which she finally quitted for her last journey to Winchester, May 23, 1817. The intervening seventeen months brought severe trial and distress to all the George Austens. Henry was declared a bankrupt in March, 1816, having only just recovered, in January, 1815, from a three months' illness, in the course of which his life had been despaired of. Jane had nursed him all the time, at the expense, as her relations afterwards believed, of her own health and strength. These began to fail her, and she consulted a physician in London before returning home, not yet as an avowed, but as an incipient, invalid, who was depending more and more exclusively upon her immediate family for society.[1]

She scarcely left her home after this return, but she once paid a visit to old friends in Berkshire (who noticed with concern that a change had taken place in her health and bearing), and she once went to Cheltenham in the vain hope of deriving benefit from its waters. Cheltenham is the only place where she might have fallen in with Dr. Smyth after ' Emma ' was published ; but if such a meeting occurred her state of depression and weakness makes it doubly unlikely she would lay a trap for a friend such as she had denounced many years before in one of her earliest books. We can only conclude that whoever may have attempted to deceive Dr. Smyth in this way it could not at any time, and least of all at that time, have been Jane Austen, who never had anything in common with the tricks of the Miss Steeles or the hoydenish manners of Lydia Bennet. Collect-

[1] *Life and Letters*, Chap. XX.

ing the opinions of those who read her novels was a great entertainment to her, and there is a long list of such verdicts, both good and bad, on ' Emma ' given in her biography.[1] In this list Dr. Smyth's name does not appear. It is, however, possible that an attempt to obtain his opinion, in the manner described above, was made by some common friend, so intimately acquainted with Dr. Smyth as to make the artifice appear permissible, since it would relate to a third person only.

At the close of the original ' Memoir ' its author, after correcting a complete mistake made by Miss Mitford respecting Jane Austen which she had given on her mother's authority, adds these words which may very well be quoted here : ' All persons who undertake to narrate from hearsay things which are supposed to have taken place before they were born, are liable to error, and are apt to call in imagination to the aid of memory : and hence it arises that many a fancy piece has been substituted for genuine history.'

[1] *Life and Letters*, Chap. XVIII.

CHARADES

WRITTEN A HUNDRED YEARS AGO BY JANE
AUSTEN AND HER FAMILY

IT is hoped that these old-fashioned charades and
conundrums possess a degree of merit sufficient to
afford entertainment to any persons inclined to take
pleasure in this kind of amusement, and, more
especially, that they may interest that inner circle
of readers who love the name of Jane Austen.

It is not as a celebrated writer that she appears
in these pages, but as one of a family group gathered
round the fireside at Steventon Rectory, Chawton
Manor House, or Godmersham Park, to enliven the
long evenings of a hundred years ago by merry
verses and happy, careless inventions of the moment,
such as flowed without difficulty from the lively minds
and ready pens of those amongst whom she lived.

Three of these charades are by Jane herself, and
even if her name did not appear beneath them their
authorship might possibly have been apparent to
those already acquainted with the playful exaggera-
tions and sparkling nonsense in which she sometimes loved to indulge when writing with perfect
unrestraint to her sister and other relations. In
all work intended for the public eye these had to
be kept within due bounds ; we find nothing but

the soberest decorum in the charade laid long ago
upon the table at Hartfield, and transcribed by
Emma into that thin quarto of hot-pressed paper
in which Harriet was making ' her only mental
provision for the evening of life.'

The habit of writing charades seems to have
been general in the Austen family. Only one by her
father survives, but there are several by her mother,
Cassandra Leigh by birth, who was well gifted with—
to use a term of her own—' sprack wit.' Cassandra's
brother, James Leigh, who inherited the estate of
North Leigh in Oxfordshire from the Perrots, and
added their name to his own, was noted in the family
as a writer of good charades, and four of his lead
the way in this little collection. They may have
been composed by him in his young days at Bath,
in which gay and fashionable resort he and his wife
were often to be found, or at his country home,
Scarlets, in Berkshire, where as an older man he
passed most of his time.

All the other charades come from the pens of
three generations of Austens, and are inserted
according to the ages of the writers. Next in order
to the charades by Jane's parents come those of
her eldest brother, James, who on his father's death
succeeded to the family living of Steventon, Hants ;
then one by her brother Henry, a brilliant, versatile
member of the family party. The next is by her
sister, her second self, Cassandra ; and the succeeding
one by Francis, the elder of her two sailor brothers,
who survived all the rest of his generation and died
as Sir Francis Austen, Admiral of the Fleet, in 1865,

aged ninety-two. Jane's own charades follow next in order. Two of her brothers are not represented here, Edward Austen, afterwards Edward Knight, and Charles, the youngest of the family. The last two charades are by a nephew, who, being nearly nineteen at the time of her death in July, 1817, and well able to use his pen before that time, can claim a place among the Steventon writers, even though his charades may possibly date from the comparatively modern period of only seventy or eighty years ago.

The key to No. 5, the only one of her father's we possess, was long lost, and many accomplished charade-guessers tried in vain to recover the meaning, which he had hidden with much graceful subtilty. It was at last discovered not very long ago by his great-great-grandson, the late William Chambers Lefroy, Esq., of Goldings, Basingstoke.

The accompanying portraits are taken from family miniatures. That of Jane Austen and the engraving of her home at Steventon Rectory are reproduced, by the kind permission of Mr. Richard Bentley, from her Memoir published by his father in 1870. Most sincere thanks are due to Miss Ellen G. Hill, of Inverleith House, Hampstead, to whose talent and kindness we owe the illustrations she has been so good as to furnish for two of the charades. Our gratitude is only increased by the knowledge that it has been to her, in every sense of the words, a labour of love.

June, 1895.

I

Two brothers, wisely kept apart, together are employed.
Though to one purpose both are bent, each takes a different side.
To us nor heads nor mouths belong, yet plain our tongues appear,
With them we never speak a word, without them useless are.
In blood and wounds we deal, yet good in temper we are proved ;
We are from passion always free, yet oft in anger moved.
We travel much, yet prisoners are, and close confined to boot,
Can with the swiftest horse keep pace, yet always go on foot.

JAMES LEIGH PERROT.

II

A HEAD and mouth I have, but—what's the wonder—
My head and mouth are very far asunder.
In at my mouth each day what I receive,
Without emetics, back again I give.
Eyes I have none, yet never miss my way ;
I have no legs, yet quickly run away.
With one hint more enough will sure be said,
I always travel, always keep my bed.

JAMES LEIGH PERROT.

THE WATCH.

III

In confinement I'm chained every day,
  Yet my enemies need not be crowing,
To my chain I have always a key,
  And no prison can keep me from going.

Small and weak are my hands I allow,
  Yet for striking my character's great.
Though ruined by one fatal blow,
  My strokes, if hard pressed, I repeat.

I have neither mouth, eye, nor ear,
  Yet I always keep time as I sing,
Change of season I never need fear,
  Though my being depends on the spring.

Would you wish, if these hints are too few,
  One glimpse of my figure to catch?
Look round! I shall soon be in view
  If you have but your eyes on the watch.

JAMES LEIGH PERROT

IV

Though low is my station,
  The Chief in the Nation
On me for support oft depend;
  Young and old, strong and weak,
  My assistance all seek,
Yet all turn their backs on their friend.

M

At the first rout in Town
Every Duchess will own
My company not a disgrace;
Yet at each rout you'll find
I am still left behind,
And to everyone forced to give place.

Without bribe or treat,
I have always a seat
In the Chapel so famed of St. Stephen;
There I lean to no side,
With no party divide,
But keep myself steady and even.

Each debate I attend
From beginning to end,
Yet I seem neither weary nor weaker;
In the house every day
Not a word do I say,
Yet in me you behold a good speaker.

JAMES LEIGH PERROT.

V

WITHOUT me, divided, fair ladies, I ween,
At a ball or a concert you'll never be seen,
You must do me together, or safely I'd swear,
Whatever your carriage, you'll never get there.

GEORGE AUSTEN.

VI

SOMETIMES I am bright, sometimes covered with
   soot,
   I'm of very great use at a feast ;
I am often applied to the right or left foot ;
   I'm a Fish, I'm a Boy, I'm a Beast.

CASSANDRA AUSTEN (*Senior*).

VII

My first, when good, may claim another ;
My second water cannot smother ;
My whole stands in the way before ye,
And puts a stop to speed and hurry.

CASSANDRA AUSTEN (*Senior*).

VIII

My first implies mirth, and my second reflection.
If my whole you divide in a proper direction,
It will tell you your fortune and answer your
   question.

CASSANDRA AUSTEN (*Senior*).

M 2

IX

SINGLY to possess my charms,
Soldiers, fearless, rush to arms;
Lawyers to their briefs apply,
Politicians scheme and lie;
Disregarding toil and scars,
And when they've gained me—bless their stars !

But when joined with any other,
Though it be a very brother,
All our glory's banished quite,
We are then kept out of sight.

Modest ladies scarce will name us,
Though we made one lady famous,
Yet guess for once our name aright,
And when you find us, keep us tight.

JAMES AUSTEN.

X

IN my first, that he may not be tardy and late
My second to do, and make nobody wait,
   A curate oft crosses the plain;
But if to my whole he should ever advance,
To me it appears an improbable chance
   That he'll ever do either again.

JAMES AUSTEN.

XI

By all prudent folk he a rash man is reckoned
Who, before he has gotten my first, takes my second,
Yet my first will afford him but little delight
To the name of my whole if my second's no right.

JAMES AUSTEN.

XII

DIVIDED, of an ancient house am I
A long, and dark, and sometimes useless story ;
United, I declare the station high
Of those who best support old England's glory.

JAMES AUSTEN.

XIII

My first a horseman's dire disgrace would tell
If it were only longer by an ell ;
My next, if strong enough and not too short,
Will always prove old age's best support ;
But much I doubt if any living wight
Could well support my whole for one short night.

JAMES AUSTEN.

XIV

If there be truth in proverbs old, my first,
Though best of servants, is of masters worst ;
Ruin unlimited my second brings ;
Then, flushed with triumph, knaves exult o'er
    kings ;
My whole a different scene, more welcome, gave,
Saw kings victorious, and a vanquished knave.

JAMES AUSTEN.

XV

I with a Footboy once was curst,
Whose name when shortened made my first.
He an unruly rogue was reckoned
And in the house oft raised my second.
My whole stands high in lists of fame,
Exalting e'en great Chatham's name.

HENRY AUSTEN.

XVI

Should you chance to suffer thirst
Turn my second to my first ;
My whole is in the garden dug,
And may be fairly called a drug.

CASSANDRA ELIZABETH AUSTEN.

167]   The Young Girl of Spirit.

XVII

By my first you may travel with safety and speed,
Though many dislike the conveyance indeed ;
  My second no woman can well be.
My whole takes a change several times in a year
Hot and cold, wet and dry, benignant, severe,
  What am I, fair lady, pray tell me ?

FRANCIS WILLIAM AUSTEN.

XVIII

When my first is a task to a young girl of spirit,
  And my second confines her to finish the piece,
How hard is her fate ! but how great is her merit
  If by taking my whole she effect her release !

JANE AUSTEN.

XIX

Divided, I'm a gentleman
  In public deeds and powers ;
United, I'm a monster, who
  That gentleman devours.

JANE AUSTEN.

XX

You may lie on my first by the side of a stream,
  And my second compose to the nymph you adore,
But if, when you've none of my whole, her esteem
  And affection diminish—think of her no more !

JANE AUSTEN.

XXI

Shake my first, and to you in return it will give
  A good shake, perhaps rather too rough.
If you suffer my second a twelvemonth to live
  You will find it grown quite big enough.
My whole stands all day with its back to the wall,
  A sad gossip as ever you'll meet,
Knows the first of each robbery, concert, or ball,
  And tells every soul in the street.

JAMES EDWARD AUSTEN (LEIGH).

XXII

My first to aid the works of man
  From heaven a present came,
And yet this gift, do what he can,
  He cannot catch nor tame.

For now 'tis on the mountain's brow,
  And now 'tis on the wave,
Now sighs in Beauty's bower, and now
  Howls o'er the maniac's grave.

My second, like my first, I'm sure
From heaven its essence drew
As soft, as fragrant, and as pure ;
Say not, as changeful too !

My whole explores earth's deepest stores,
And draws exhaustless up
The purest draught that e'er is quaffed
From mortal's varying cup.

JAMES EDWARD AUSTEN (LEIGH).

WRITERS OF THE CHARADES

Rev. GEORGE AUSTEN = CASSANDRA LEIGH

JAMES LEIGH (PERROT)
Brother to
Cassandra Leigh

JAMES
AUSTEN
Eldest Son

HENRY
AUSTEN
Third Son

CASSANDRA
ELIZABETH AUSTEN
Eldest Daughter

FRANCIS
AUSTEN
Fourth Son

JANE
AUSTEN
Second Daughter

JAMES EDWARD
AUSTEN (LEIGH)

KEY

I. Pair of Spurs.

II. River.

III. Repeating Watch.

IV. Chair.

V. A Light.

VI. Jack.

VII. Turnpike.

VIII. Merry-thought.

IX. Garter(s).

X. Canterbury.

XI. Housewife.

XII. Aloft.

XIII. Falstaff.

XIV. Waterloo.*

XV. Patriot.

XVI. Liquorice.

XVII. Season.

XVIII. Hemlock.

XIX. Agent.

XX. Bank Note.

XXI. Handbill.

XXII. Windlass.

* In the game of Loo, Knaves are reckoned above Kings. One form of the game is called ' Unlimited Loo.'

Printed by SPOTTISWOODE, BALLANTYNE & CO. LTD.
Colchester, London & Eton, England.

For EU product safety concerns, contact us at Calle de José Abascal, 56–1°, 28003 Madrid, Spain or eugpsr@cambridge.org.

www.ingramcontent.com/pod-product-compliance
Ingram Content Group UK Ltd.
Pitfield, Milton Keynes, MK11 3LW, UK
UKHW012344130625
459647UK00009B/522